Mom, Dad, Me, and Classic TV

Growing up with Classic Television's Harry Ackerman and Elinor Donahue

By **Peter K. Ackerman**

BearManor Media.com

Mom, Dad, Me, and Classic TV
Copyright ©2024 Peter K. Ackerman. All Rights Reserved.

All rights reserved. Without limiting the rights under copyright reserved above, no part of this publication may be reproduced, stored in or introduced into a retrieval system, or transmitted, in any form, or by any means (electronic, mechanical, photocopying, recording, or otherwise) without the prior written permission of both the copyright owner and the above publisher of this book.

This print edition is licensed for your personal enjoyment only. This Publication may not be resold or given away to other people. If you would like to share this book with another person, please purchase an additional copy for each person you share it with. Thank you for respecting the author's work.

Disclaimer: All content presented under this title was gained from common and reputable sources in both print and online. If any details within this title are found to be incorrect, the author apologizes and will be happy to make corrections in the next edition.

Typesetting and layout by PKJ Passion Global

Published in the USA by
BearManor Media
1317 Edgewater Dr #110
Orlando FL 32804
www.BearManorMedia.com

Softcover Edition
ISBN-10:
ISBN-13: 979-8-88771-389-2

Published in the USA by Bear Manor Media

To Marie, Harry, and Amy –
each and all of you make life complete.

Table of Contents

Acknowledgements

This book could not, of course, be written without my mom and dad, Harry Ackerman and Elinor Donahue. For their career choices and taking me along to the studio, thank you! My mother, with whom I speak by phone almost every week, and my stepfather, Louis Genevrino, are wonderful supporters and a great couple.

Thank you to my own family, Marie, my spouse of over 35 years, and our children Harry and Amy, who patiently either heard me tell many of the stories countless times or encouraged me through this process.

There are many others to thank who were part of the journey to publishing this memoir. Herbie J. Pilato, an author on plenty of media topics, was a great encouragement from the beginning. As I shared anecdotes on social media, he not only said, "Peter, you have got to put these in a book!" but he also put me in touch with my literary agent. Finally, he was my brainstorming partner over the title of the work. I am grateful to him on so many levels.

Diane Nine is the literary agent extraordinaire! From the get-go, she took me figuratively by the hand and led me through the arduous process that is writing. Through Diane I met Kyle Linkous who read through an early draft and helped me understand where I could add material. It was from her feedback that I feel I found my "voice" in this book.

Of course, I could not have produced the book if not for Jodi Lyons, a talented author who joined my project and helped me get it to its finished form in good time. Jodi made herself available to me and was always good about helping me to understand the writing process.

To my publisher and those who work at BearManor Publishing, I appreciate all the work that went on to get my humble work published among your other fabulous books.

There are many friends who encouraged me over time and with this project. Just a few include "Sam" Faeth, Jennifer Groht, and Beth Beardsley, the latter who provided me helpful feedback over many early drafts of my manuscript.

There are also the locations where I spent time focusing on this project away from home and work. To the staff and patrons of Stogies in Lodi, California and Leonardtown Cigars in Leonardtown, Maryland, thank you for providing a place that offered a cool and relaxed vibe, where a club soda sipping novice author could get some composition work accomplished.

To the worship communities I have been associated with, some are where my show business anecdotes became part of sermons, and other parishes from where the people encouraged me to write, a big thank you to Immanuel Church on the Hill, Alexandria Virginia; St. Christopher's Episcopal Church, Springfield, VA; The Episcopal Church of St. John the Baptist, Lodi, California; and Christ Church King Queen Parish, Chaptico Maryland.

Finally, I thank God for a, thus far, delightful, adventurous life that has taken me from the ups and downs of show business, particularly classic television, and led me to a vocation like no other.

Introduction

Have you ever sat in front of the television and wished that you were living in Mayberry, or sitting around the Cleaver family's dinner table, or helping Tarzan navigate his latest adventure? Like many children at a young age, I certainly imagined that growing up, and figured I'm not alone in those dreams. Since today's TV lineup features multiple new cable channels devoted solely to the genre of Classic Television, it seems that many viewers wish they could return to a simpler time in television, where the scandal of the neighborhood was the woman with the twitchy nose whose family seemed to experience an awful lot of unexplained things.

Of course, except for perhaps taking a trip to a movie theme park, it is all but impossible to enter the imaginary world of Classic Television, but my experience came close. My father was Harry Ackerman, the Executive Producer of such shows as *Bewitched*, *The Flying Nun*, *Hazel*, *Dennis the Menace*, and *Gidget* (to name a few). My mother is Elinor Donahue, the actress who starred in shows such as *Father Knows Best*, *The Andy Griffith Show*, *The Odd Couple*, guest-starred on programs ranging from Star *Trek: The Original Series* to *Friends,* and appeared in films like *Pretty Woman*.

I was born into the world of Classic Television, and I grew up surrounded by its stars, frolicked on its sets, and enjoyed one-of-a-kind experiences and exciting adventures along the way. Though I first followed in each of my parent's footsteps; first as an actor, and later in production for television commercials, music videos, and television, I finally found my way to a whole new vocation that's far from show business. Yet, what I learned from my parents is invaluable, and I still use that knowledge each day of my life. For instance, I'm one of those few people who actually enjoys being in front of others. I know that preparing for presentations is just as important as executing them. And frankly, it has never hurt in my vocation to have some interesting show business-related stories to help illustrate points I'm attempting to make.

Chapter 1

Hollywood Be Thy Name

"Our Father, who art in heaven…HOLLYWOOD…be thy name." With my father an Executive Producer and mother an actress, it's no wonder they held smiles back night after night as they encouraged us to pray before bed. Like many families at that time, we practiced religious observance on Sundays, but the rest of the week was focused on work. In a sense, they worked for the "town factory," also known famously as show business.

Growing up in the 1960s through the mid-1980s, I was given the special experience of seeing how my parents evolved into the medium of television, watching as it developed before their eyes. I saw how they handled the joys, upheavals, and trials that came with the ever-changing television industry. My upbringing didn't seem unique to me at the time, but I realize now that visiting the set of *Bewitched*, standing on the bridge of the Star Ship Enterprise, and later—when I worked in production—standing in for Steven Tyler while the rest of Aerosmith practiced for a music video shoot, are not what you would call ordinary childhood memories. So, here we go. If you are willing, please come with me as I take you through the journey of growing up in a show business family and give you a glimpse of what it was like to live within this grand time in Classic Television history.

Long before I attended the 1985 Walk of Fame Ceremony where my dad received his very own star on the famous sidewalk; before I was working at Warner Bros. and wandered onto a stage only to find my mother rehearsing with actor Elliott Gould for their guest roles on an episode of *Friends*; before I would work in the production office for two seasons on that series, I knew the two famous figures – Harry Ackerman and Elinor Donahue – as simply Mom and Dad.

You are probably familiar with my parents based on the television shows of your youth, or perhaps you have encountered them in those same, now "older," "cleaner" shows being rerun on cable channels. In the smoke emanating from the animated frying pan near the conclusion of the opening credits of *Bewitched* (1964-1972) or over Sally Field during the opening credits of *The Flying Nun* (1967-1979) as she flies in white nun's garb, you might recall seeing the title across the television screen: "Executive Producer – Harry Ackerman." Or perhaps you have seen Elinor Donahue as the iconic Betty Anderson, the eldest sibling of the fictional family on *Father Knows Best* (1954-1960). You might remember her as Ellie Walker, the pharmacist, during the first season of *The Andy Griffith Show* (1960-1968); as a character on a key episode of *Star Trek: The Original Series* (1966-1968); or playing Felix Unger's girlfriend in *The Odd Couple* (1970-1975). Movie fans may recognize her as the nice sales lady, Bridget, who helps Julia Roberts in *Pretty Woman* (1990). For my parents, these are just a few roles performed in an ordinary day.

Growing up in Hollywood was and is a great thing and provided a jackpot of memories. I frequently share these gifts in my sermons and stories. As I prepare to do so now with you, let me first lay the groundwork and introduce you to my parents.

Who is Harry Ackerman?

My dad generally stood firmly in the present. Thus, I know about what I experienced with him, but not so much about his past. Though he might occasionally share about an event or a person, he did not liberally offer stories about his growing up. Since I was in my 20s when he died, it never occurred to me to ask him. The fun part about this situation is I continually become surprised by discovery, as I learn more about my dad. Perhaps one day an author will compose a scholarly biography on Harry Ackerman. For now, the reader has me, certainly not an historian on the television industry. What follows is what I know.

Every day people stride along Hollywood Boulevard, the warm California sun lighting up the way, and warming them, as the sound of usually heavy car traffic is part of the background. Daily, in this downtown city atmosphere, individuals look before them at the names encased in stars on the Walk of Fame. I wonder if, as tourists move west on Hollywood Boulevard heading toward Cherokee Ave past Musso & Frank's Bar and Grill, they suddenly look down and see the name there and say in response "Harry Ackerman, who is he?" Harry Ackerman was one of the people responsible for putting *I Love Lucy* (1951-1957) on the air. He was also the Executive Producer on many television programs and worked with many stars. Whether in his radio days or television ones, my dad was once a player in the industry, and one of the few who made enough of a mark to be memorialized on the sidewalk. He was one of those fortunate creators, and I get to join alongside many others who are still proud to this day of him and his accomplishments.

Born in 1912, the year the Titanic sank, my dad spent his childhood in Albany, New York. The son of Dutch and Irish parents, his mother was a Flannery, and his father came from a long line of Ackermans, Americanized over time from the Dutch "Ucherman." Because of the history of the Albany Dutch, and the fact that they likely cohabitated with the Mohawk Native Americans, my dad hopefully assumed that his ability to tan so well had to do with the fact that we had indigenous blood in us. A true explanation came from Harry's aunt, opera singer Mary Mellish, who wrote in her autobiography *Sometimes I Reminisce* that the darker pigmentation was most likely to do with what is called "Black Irish." She wrote, "My parents, grandparents, sisters, brothers, and now the young generation are more Spanish in coloring. I have long suspected that some young gallants from the Spanish Armada made successful conquests among my Irish ancestors."[1]

---

1   G.P. Putnam's Sons, copyright 1941, p. 9

What do I know about my dad from his boyhood? The only artifacts I have from that period of his life are books he read in his pre-teenage years. These musty hardcover books with yellowing pages sit on my bookshelf today. These fictional boys' novels are all about adventure which suggests to me that my dad had an adventurous spirit from a young age. My dad, when I knew him, lived fully and joyfully in the moment. While leaning towards the future, he rarely looked back. This trait certainly assisted him in his climb to success, but the negative aspect for my siblings and me is that he never talked much about his pre-California days. What I do know from him about his early years was told as adventure stories he read to us at night.

On more than one occasion when recounting his past, my dad talked of his rebellious period. He ran away from home and "eventually fell in with the wrong crowd." He ventured first to New York City, hiding in a movie theatre until discovered by the management and thrown out. But before he was caught, he'd repeatedly watched The Marx Bros. film, *The Cocoanuts* (1929). I could think of worse films to continuously watch! Little did he know that many years later he would have personal stories, good and bad, about two of the famed brothers.

After that small sanctuary was torn away, young adventurer Harry Ackerman hit the streets, which eventually led him into police custody before he was returned to his family. With life on the road not being as romantic as he imagined, he was placed into Christian Brothers Academy, a boarding school where my dad finally applied himself to his studies. With his scholastic accomplishments and the fact that his mother came from an influential family, the young teenager was able to get into Dartmouth where he majored in English. However, this period soon turned bleak when news hit my dad that his own father, Harold Ackerman, had committed suicide. All I ever knew about my grandfather was someone once describing him to me as a quiet and distant person. I wonder if Grandfather Ackerman struggled with demons of depression or alcoholism.

Regardless, I will never know why my father did not share stories about his own dad.

Still, life continued as an adventure and my father navigated the ride. He became involved in college theater and in at least one year supervised his class's snow statue, in an annual contest that had students creating and building in the frigid New Hampshire air.

After graduation, it seemed fate intervened when one of my dad's classmates offered him a job on a new comedy radio show that was going to be broadcast from New York City. This was his first step into the business that eventually would lead to his receiving a star on Hollywood Boulevard. Soon after, young Harry Ackerman, in his 20's, was wooed by a fellow Dartmouth alum, Pat Weaver, an advertising executive who would later become the President of NBC. It was through his relationship with Mr. Weaver that my dad began working at Young & Rubicam advertising in various positions, mostly overseeing radio program production. This period included, as I understand it, my dad actually directing radio episodes of *The Lone Ranger* (1933-1956) whose sponsor was handled by the agency. When not directing, Dad lived in his New York apartment with his bridge-playing mother and was able to walk and explore the city and the sights, which were impressive in the middle- to late-1930s, also known as the post-Depression and post-Prohibition period. He kept his 5'11" frame to 150 lbs. by walking to meetings and to the usual two martini lunches that were the norm of that period. He was a regular smoker. Life was good, and he entered into a new stage of life, marriage.

About his courtship and marriage to actress Mary Shipp, I know nothing. The household I grew up in was with a mother who was my dad's second wife. Propriety was a mark of my dad, whom many people referred to as a true gentleman. This reason was probably why he did not share anything about his first marriage. Suffice it to say, his marriage to Mary in 1939 did not help with his own family. Their nuptials happened in a time where there were some, like this extended family in Albany New York, who looked askance at someone in their clan marrying an actress. No doubt, this attitude did not help when later, he married my mother when he was twenty-five years her senior! Mary and my dad eventually moved to the West Coast when my dad was hired by CBS.

My paternal grandmother, whom I know very little about as her death preceded my birth, was a sickly woman who lived with them when they moved to California. At some point during dad's marriage to Mary, his mother, Anna Flannery Ackerman, died.

Though I am not fully clear on the vocational and personal timelines, he and Mary, unable to conceive, adopted two children, Stephen and Susan: more about them later.

On both the East Coast and West Coast, my dad concentrated his talents on the broadcasting medium of radio. There are a couple of stories that he shared with me. Once, when correcting young Mickey Rooney over a line reading, the actor decided he was going to fight my dad. Though Rooney's "Irish" was up, his friend, young Judy Garland who was also on the program, was able to hold Mickey back. When he recounted this episode, my dad said he never took Rooney's desire to hit him too seriously if Judy could so easily stop him.

Orson Welles and my dad knew one another. He is one of my favorite personalities, and so I love the fact that my dad and Welles have a story I can share. Besides acting and directing, Mr. Welles also read poetry as part of a daily CBS radio show that my father oversaw. Dad told me about the time he was in the booth for a show that was broadcast from the Los Angeles studios in early December 1941. The station received the news of the Pearl Harbor bombing. There was a scurry to find someone to make the first report of the tragedy, but with no news person immediately available, they had to look to pull someone currently available from the on-air group. To Harry, Orson Welles seemed like the obvious choice. Yet, he told me that there was some back-and-forth between him and the other executives. Only a few years previously, on the same network, Welles enjoyed his *War of the Worlds*

Halloween prank. Consequently, on the day of the Pearl Harbor bombing, some in the radio station production booth, with the smell of coffee and cigarettes wafting around the tense space, pondered, "Will listeners take Welles seriously, delivering such unbelievable news?" My dad made the decision and insisted that Welles make the announcement. He recalled that Orson was the perfect choice to deliver the dramatic, tragic news, and did so with authority and sincerity.

Besides Orson Welles, Judy Garland, and Mickey Rooney, my dad worked with all kinds of stars in his radio days, which I know about not from stories he told, but from a cache of photos taken at the time. The personalities he worked with include such classic luminaries of the silver screen as Clark Gable, Myrna Loy, and Edward Arnold, to name a few. His close proximity to celebrity extended beyond his vocation. He was drinking and dining buddies with a couple known in the press at the time as the "Battling Bogarts" -- Humphrey Bogart and his then wife Mayo Methot; named for their very public booze-fueled fights. It seems to me that my father was living the life. He was well-known, appreciated, and was making his mark not only in the field of radio, but also in the ever-developing television market.

Part of his promotion at CBS that brought him and Mary to Los Angeles, California had him figuratively working alongside William H. Paley, the President of CBS who was on the East Coast. Mr. Paley made my dad become the West Coast representative of the company as the Vice President. At first, my dad began overseeing creative input for many talents including: Eve Arden in *Our Miss Brooks* (1948-1957 on radio, 1952-1956 on television), where she played a high school teacher in this situation comedy; and Richard Denning and Lucille Ball in *My Favorite Husband* (1948-1951), the precursor show on radio which later became *I Love Lucy*. Later, his contributions led him into supervising the television arm of the company, which included transitioning many of these radio programs into television shows.

While essentially serving as the West Coast president of the network, my father contributed to television, along with others, in bringing about the "three camera technique" that is still in use today. The names associated with the development of this style of using three cameras at once to record the action on the set change depending on who reports it. Some of those involved claim to be the one, but my dad recalled that it was a group decision, which I later saw confirmed in a piece written in an Emmy Magazine editorial. Desi Arnaz, William "Bill" Paley of CBS, Jess Oppenheimer, and Al Simon have all laid claim to inventing the technique, but my dad held, and history holds the clues, that this was a meeting of the minds of many. Both Al Simon and my dad had worked together on productions before *I Love Lucy*. My dad in his role in CBS oversaw the televised game show *Truth or Consequences* (1941-*1975)* and the television series *Amos 'n Andy* (1951-1955). Al Simon also worked on these shows, and it appears that both programs used, at least occasionally, multiple cameras. This leads me to believe that my dad, Mr. Simon, and the others who worked on *I Love Lucy* shared some knowledge on the technology available to them and collaborated on how it could be applied to their situation with Lucy needing the reaction of an audience.

On *I Love Lucy*, the nexus of the discussion was around Lucille Ball's comedic timing. She honed her talent as a comedienne doing her character on the late 1940s radio show, *My Favorite Husband*. Now that it was a television show, her comedy timing was off. The group—Harry, Desi, Jess, Al, and others—realized that Lucy needed the audience that the radio studio offered, but the television counterpart did not. Most who knew her understood that Lucy's comedy worked so well on a radio series because she had a live audience from which she could gauge the laughter. It allowed her to adjust her performance according to the audience's response. Her excellent sense of timing, and her ability to thrive as a comedienne, depended on her having an audience. One only needs to watch her doing, "Vitameatavegamin" or the candy on the conveyor belt to see how easy she makes it look. In reality, she takes the comedic magic to the next level towards the outrageous when appropriate, and then pulls it back as the audience's exclamations die down. Lucille Ball was brilliant, and the people behind the cameras helped to support her talent. Supporting others on the set was a large part of who my dad was as a professional.

In short, he worked well with others. That characteristic was at the heart of who he was. In the biography *Lucille: The Life of Lucille Ball* by Kathleen Brady, the author wrote, "He [Harry Ackerman] was that rare corporate individual who believed that ushers were as worthy of his notice as executives (p.182)."[2] This is the man who I saw in action later in life when I joined him at the studio.

The timeline between his many contributions as Vice-President of West Coast Production at CBS and becoming an Executive Producer is something I do not know. I grew up in a household where I saw my dad's name as the Executive Producer on television programs such as *The Donna Reed Show*, *Bachelor Father*, *Leave It To Beaver*, *Dennis the Menace*, *Gidget*, *Bewitched*, *Hazel*, and *The Flying Nun*. As a boy, after he told me that he once worked for CBS, I asked him why he became a producer. He informed me that he liked the process of creating that occurred in an ongoing series, and decided to move into that role, which led him to many contributions to the medium over time.

Besides his contributions to television, I suspect my dad was instrumental in developing a tool, not used as much today, but one that he was never without. My father popularized a pocket notecard known as "buck slips." With his light blue felt tip pen, he constantly made notes, but finding the right card size frustrated him. He discovered the solution to his search one day when he ventured into a tiny stationery/print shop on Little Santa Monica Boulevard. ("Just east of Beverly Drive and on the north side of the street," my mother

---

2   *Lucille: The Life of Lucille Ball*, Kathleen Brady, Hyperion, New York, 1994, p. 182

recalls). There he found blank cards offered on a dollar bill stock size. The reason for his specificity is that these buck slips fit perfectly into any of the upper pockets on a man's suit coat or shirt. From there, he ordered a personalized set to be created for him. He had the printer place the word "Memo" at the top and his name along the bottom. Shortly thereafter, as my dad handed out notes to people, and as family legend goes, these "Harry Ackerman-buck slips" got noticed by other show business executives and not long after, every studio's print shop was creating the same buck slips for others. Even today, filmmaker/podcaster/comedian Adam Corolla swears by and uses his own version of what he refers to as "buck slips."

While my dad thrived professionally, his marriage did not. My dad and Mary experienced martial problems and separated. They officially divorced in 1961, which added another nail to the coffin that buried the relationship with his East Coast family. The Ackermans of Albany New York were strict Roman-Catholics. If there was one thing worse than someone of their stature marrying a "lowly" (in their eyes) actress, it was divorce. My only interaction with Mary was at my dad's funeral when I stood in line to receive condolences and she came through. A few years before then, I remember my dad escorting me out of a grocery store when he saw that his ex-wife walked in. Those experiences are all I can say about the state of their relationship. After they separated, I understand that Mary took over most of the child-rearing responsibilities, while Dad paid child support and remained active and present in his children's lives.

His divorce from Mary, coupled with the death of his loving, but at times, I understand, domineering mother, set the stage for the next chapter of Harry's life. This intersecting road began in 1937 when a child was born in Tacoma, Washington who would be just as much a representative of Classic Television as Harry.

Beginning Life as Mary Eleanor Donahue

My mother and I are close. I was also very close to her mother, my grandmother, and the only grandparent in my family whom I ever knew, Doris Donahue, whom I knew as Nana. Unlike with my dad, I have a lot more stories about my mom's early years. She was born Mary Eleanor Donahue in Tacoma, Washington in 1937 and was the youngest child to my grandmother and Thomas Donahue. Thomas was a not-too-friendly father; distant, and with a roving eye for other women. Mr. Donahue left Doris for another woman, leaving my grandmother to fend for herself in order to make the family's ends meet. Being a thrifty woman her whole life, she spent carefully and saved money as she could. She knew how to sew, how to cook, how to clean, and wasn't afraid to work. She worked in a candy shop and for various seamstress companies over the years. Doris scraped enough together to survive. She remained closely and geographically connected to my mother for the rest of her life. There was a deep connection between my grandmother and mom, no doubt created by the rough times they experienced while making ends meet, as well as when Elinor's, at that time known as Mary Eleanor, show business career began at a young age.

My mom was in a dance class with her older sister at Reitha Geary's Dance Studio, located in a high-rise building in Tacoma, Washington. That same space housed the local radio station KOMO-Seattle. The station somehow got word that Mary Eleanor could, by the age of two, dance and sing very well. Since KOMO had a Saturday morning show called *Youth Makes a Record*, they put my mother on the air one week. Positive feedback resulted in Mary Eleanor Donahue being invited periodically to do repeat radio appearances. This prompted her, at the ripe age of two, to need a Social Security Card, well before other people attained theirs. My mom could not sign her own name, which was a requirement in having the card. My mother recalls this early time in her life, saying, "I still have my original card, dated 1939. Because I had to officially sign it myself, and could not, because I was two, my mother placed her hand over mine and 'guided' my first handwritten signature." Some of her singing work at KOMO was actually recorded, and she owns those 78 records from the broadcasts.

Continuing in 1939, she was performing as a member of a touring vaudeville circuit. Mary Eleanor caught the eyes of Hollywood types, and she was brought in for her first role at the age of 7 in the film—mostly unknown today, though she is completely adorable in it—*Mister Big* (1943) starring Donald O'Connor. The production was a lovely first film experience for her. She had such a crush on O'Connor that when he bounded over to meet her, she broke down in tears! A wild, unknown fact was that her character's name was Muggsy and that also happened to be a nickname of hers back home in Tacoma, Washington. Her friendship with the stars of the film, which also included Peggy Ryan, remained tight until they each passed away.

Still, with her being so young, there was much for her to learn about movies basics. For instance, when her mother brought them to the premiere of *Mister Big,* Mary Eleanor began to cry outside of the Pantages Theater in Hollywood. When asked what was wrong, she fretted that she couldn't remember the dance routine and wasn't sure she could do it again. Unaware that once film is recorded and processed it didn't need performing again, she was able to relax when she discovered all she had to do that night was watch. She was given rave reviews for the film and was soon after placed under contract at MGM. Though she did mostly B MGM films, some of those unseen for years, she was cast in two films at that studio, *The Unfinished Dance* (1947) and *Three Daring Daughters* (1948), still accessible today, which began unfolding the talents of this young actress; all presented in the glorious Technicolor of the time.

I love watching *Three Daring Daughters*. There is a key musical sequence where Powell, my mother, and others are all singing to and with Jeanette MacDonald who is recovering in bed. They sing *The Dickie Bird Song* which was a popular tune at the time. My mother sings a brief solo, and though I swear I hear her voice, she insists that her singing part was dubbed in with the voice of another performer. Since this was before my time, I have to trust my mother's recollection, though I will always hope that mine is right. Just seeing her at nine years old in glorious MGM technicolor is a treat I get to cherish!

Something that also took center stage in these films, that probably went unnoticed to viewers, is a phrase my mother so lovingly defined as the "Donahue Squint." She recalls how bright lights caused her eyes to almost fully shut, a trait that I share with her.

While at MGM, Mary Eleanor went to the studio school with various other co-stars, including child actors who were under contract to MGM at the time, Margaret O'Brien, Elizabeth Taylor, Claude Jarman, Jr., and Gigi Perreau. In addition to the "traditional" subjects, the studio school also taught acting, singing, and dancing. During this time, although the studio had numerous young people under contract, few remained more than a year and even fewer emerged from that studio system into later film or television roles. Yet, there was something that made this studio schooling a bonding experience, creating this quality of comradery in those who went through the studio school system.

It was always a treat when I could meet my mother's contemporaries from these earlier years. My opportunities came when celebrity autograph shows began so that fans could meet and obtain signatures from their favorite personalities. Before these signing shows became regular occurrences, my mom was generous when responding to written requests for signatures. Even when our family had financial struggles, she was pleased to have fans. When they asked for a photo, she would provide the picture, sign it as requested, put it into a mailing envelope with a picture-size piece of cardboard to prevent bending, and mail it off to the recipient. Most of the time, she paid all of the packaging and postal costs associated with this star-to-fan gesture. For a brief period, she tried to get out of the regular signing circuit, even when events promised reimbursement for personal costs she had dealt out previously. Having been in this scene since she was a little girl, she was just exhausted and had ceased doing these kinds of appearances. However, at times she made rare exceptions. This is why I am glad to have seen my mother situated next to Margaret O'Brien at a celebrity signing event she decided to attend.

She and Margaret played best friends in Margaret's film, *The Unfinished Dance*, which was the first film for Danny Thomas, who played O'Brien's father. Yet, at the autograph show, my mother and Margaret remained stoically professional ; saying, "hi" politely and then focusing on meeting fans and signing pictures. There was never any tension between the two, they just had a fairly casual relationship. Sitting down at a convention where people were wanting signatures was just like sitting next to a long-time neighbor. It wasn't new, exciting, or different; for them it just was. For me, though, it was exciting to see others with whom my mother worked.

The Unfinished Dance plot segues into providing the opportunity to shed a little light on Doris Donahue and the kind of stage mother that she was. Or, more accurately in fact, wasn't. Doris used to tell the story about how the film's director, Henry Koster, was not having a particularly fun production day during an early sequence featuring the dance class where dozens of girls, including Mary Eleanor and Margaret O'Brien, were being taken through their ballet positions. Apparently when filming this sequence, the "stage mothers," which was the lovingly official name for the parents and guardians of underage youth, had their chairs seated nearby the director. Not only were they correcting their children between the shots, with phrases like, "turn this way, not that," they would also attempt to give the gifted director ideas, which of course, would benefit their child. Finally, the director had them removed from the set. "Why can you not be more like Mrs. Donahue?" Where was she? Crocheting! Sitting in an unused portion of the set. She knew not to get involved and to let the director do what the director did; direct. She let her daughter do what she was there to do, dance. Doris knew that her contribution would be to stay out of the way.

It was while in rehearsals for *The Unfinished Dance* that my mother's stint at MGM was extended to a long-term contract. One day during rehearsals, she looked over and saw the film's producer,

Joe Pasternak, in conference with a short, well-dressed man wearing glasses, while looking at her. It was later, after they left, that she learned the shorter man was the president of Metro Goldwin Mayer Studios, Louis B. Mayer. As she later wrote in her book, "[t]hat began the happiest years of my young life." [3]

She continued to work at MGM and did quite a number of films, although none became as memorable as *The Unfinished Dance* and *Three Daring Daughters*. Eventually, her contract was dropped, and while she entered into her pre-teenage years, she faced an age conundrum that most actors will face. She had aged out of child roles but wasn't quite mature enough for the young woman roles directors were looking for. In the meantime, she took what work she could get cast in, whether that be a one-off role on television's *Playhouse 90* (1956-1960) or another show. She spent this time studying dance and her mother kept making money in any way she could. For a while, Doris worked as a seamstress at a company that was awarded a huge costume contract. She was making costumes from large animal characters, to princesses, and other fantasy beings. One day, a representative from the company they were making the costumes for came in and offered an opportunity to own shares in the company if anyone wished. I'm not sure if anyone took this man's offer, but Doris explained that she just couldn't risk money like that. It was taking everything she was making at the time to pay the rent and put food on the table in her home as a single mother. Later in life, as she has told me, she so wished she could go back and talk to her young self, because the man who had offered that chance was a representative from the little, soon-to-be opened park, Disneyland.

Elinor in Hollywood

As she grew into a teenager and young adult, my mother, still Mary Eleanor Donahue, celebrated with another significant change. While

---

3   *In the Kitchen* with Elinor Donahue, Cumberland House, Nashville TN, 1998, p. 49

perusing a periodical, she came across an article on British novelist and screenwriter Elinor Glyn. Mom fell in love with the idea of a less formal name, and after discussing it with her mother, the change was made. It was then that Mary Eleanor Donahue became Elinor Donahue.

No longer under contract to MGM, she continued to find work as a dancer, and for a while, after she was cast in *Her First Romance* (1951) with Margaret O'Brien, she even experimented with becoming a blonde. The hair color lasted only a couple of years before she went back to her natural color.

She and my grandmother did their best to keep moving forward. Nana found work at May Company while my mother, with an occasional film here and there, continued with dance lessons and professional events. According to the story that my grandmother recollected to me, it was during this time in her life that Elinor was approached by Chico Marx, and not in the most comfortable way. Mom was 16 years old and dancing in the chorus for the Annual Los Angeles Police Show held at the Shrine Auditorium. Being as she was the shortest, it was natural for her to be situated at one of the ends of the line of singers and dancers. Her place was closest to the wing at stage left (the left side of the stage as one looks at it from the audience's position) where the performers would enter from to perform. Many stars were present that day. My mother remembers Bob Hope commenting admirably about the shape of her nose. Additionally, Frank Sinatra and Chico Marx were on the bill. It's relevant to note that though many say the name of this Marx brother as, "Cheeko," it was in fact pronounced "Chick-O," and for a good reason. As I heard Groucho once comment on a radio show interview that his brother's sobriquet was apt because he was a "chicken chaser." To clarify, Lawrence J. Epstein, the author of *The Haunted Smile,* a book about Jewish comedians, reveals the name was given to him because of his known proclivity for very young girls. Chico, the actor-comedian-musician-band leader, met Elinor at the event and was talking with Doris about a film he was developing. Her daughter, he had said, seemed perfect for a part. He wondered if he might have a car and driver pick up Elinor one afternoon to chauffeur her to his home where he could work with her and prepare her for an audition. Was my grandmother perhaps too trusting in this situation, or was she just naïve? Regardless, plans were made, and my mom waited at home for the car and driver to pick her up, while her mother left for work. On her way out, my grandmother stopped by the Dance Studio where her daughter was due to have a lesson that afternoon to let them know she would be absent from the class. After my grandmother explained why, the dance instructor quickly warned her, making her aware that Chico had a reputation of luring young girls to his home with an auditioning ruse with other ideas in mind. Too far away to directly intercede, Nana phoned my mom at their home and told her to, "Shut the windows, lock the doors, hide in the house, and do not answer if anyone knocks!" The chauffeur arrived and waited for a while outside of his car. He eventually came up to the house and knocked. He tried the door, he walked around the house peering into the windows, and he eventually returned to his vehicle and honked his horn. Meanwhile, Elinor cowered quietly inside and eventually the chauffeur drove away. Though we'll never know if he was offering a true audition, I'm thankful for that phone call and the awareness that Hollywood does in fact have a darker side that unfortunately still exists today Yet, where there is darkness, light exits and breaks through. In my mother's life, despite challenges, goodness and grace existed as well.

One of the fortunate and properly familiar relationships formed was with Richard "Dick" Lane, lovingly referred to as "Daddy Dick" and his wife, whom Elinor grew to call "Auntie Esther." Elinor had been introduced to the Lanes through performances in the same vaudeville circuit. Vaudeville was a primary source of live entertainment that began touring throughout the United States in the late 1800s. Eventually, there were different producers who would package their stage shows with variety arts: ventriloquists, comedians, dancers, magicians, and the like. Though acts changed as a circuit traveled from city to city, they traversed a portion of the country for a "season." Elinor's older sister, Gwen, danced in a troupe that backed Dick Lane who was a "straight man" (the serious one) in a comedy duo. By the time Elinor was involved, Vaudeville was on its way out, but in those final days of that tour, she danced and sang in the Bert Levy Circuit which traveled the Pacific Northwest. Dick Lane, who had performed on that same circuit, remembered my grandmother, who had traveled with Gwen when he was a part of the act, and warmly invited her and her family into their lives. They became close friends, with Dick serving as a positive father figure for young Elinor. At this time, he was working in Hollywood and found steady roles in films, being a regular in the *Boston Blackie* movie series. Additionally, he was one of those wonderful, unsung character actors who seemed to appear in everything, from *Laurel & Hardy* to *Abbot & Costello* films, usually playing a fast-talking con man type. However, behind those shady roles was a very kind man. According to Elinor, he and his wife were two of the most open and generous people in Hollywood, and they all but legally adopted her as their own. Because of Mr. Lane, Elinor finally had a real father figure in her life. He was a man who cared about her, took an interest in her career, and made sure she was healthy and happy. He was a responsible family man and probably the best surrogate father she could have asked for.

After I was born, both life and professional circumstances led to the eventual drifting of this close-knit non-family-but-family group, but they were always held in high regard by Doris and Elinor. Though I never met Dick Lane, I feel as if I know him. I remember afternoons watching Roller Derby on television when Mr. Lane was the announcer. Nana would see him in action, with his fast-talking patter and say wistfully, "Oh look. It's Daddy Dick!" This was usually followed by his signature line during the Los Angeles Thunderbirds Roller Derby games: "Whoa, Nellie!"

As my mother grew up, when it came to boys, there were plenty who caught her interest. Her first crush was Peter Lawford, whom she met on the MGM lot (when she was a very young girl), and one of her first casual relationships was with a man named Jack Jones. Jack was the crooner son of film actor and operatic vocalist Alan Jones, who appeared in both Marx Brothers and Abbott & Costello films and became the iconic singer of the theme song for *The Love Boat* (1977-1987) television series.

One night, my mom and Jack went to a nightclub to see the senior Jones perform. Alas, he ended up having the most awful night on stage. He had too much to drink beforehand (he would later in life swear off alcohol), but she remembers the performance as embarrassing. She was there in support of Jack and his father on that night, and while there may have been an initial attraction, that night solidified that a friendship was what they were suited for. In the world of Hollywood performers, it's difficult for two individuals to remain completely apart. As the years went on, she and Jack bumped into each other many times, and each encounter solidified how comfortable they were as friends, despite having attempted a romantic relationship. He was probably the only man of whom my father was jealous, weirdly, due to the lack of animosity. And in a laughable twist life can often bring, it seemed that whatever event Harry and Elinor Ackerman attended, there would be Jack Jones.

I was once told the story of when my parents took off on a romantic cruise to celebrate a significant wedding anniversary. As the ship left the port, the sound of the ship's booming horn echoed in the harbor, fellow passengers tossed confetti, and my dad looked lovingly and deeply into my mother's eyes, grateful for the love that brought them this far and excited for the adventure ahead. Just as romance began to settle in, mood music began to play throughout the ship. And, of course, the music included the voice of Jones, serenading the night with the theme song to *The Love Boat*! My parents gave into the moment and laughed heartily at the fact that Jack was still in attendance, even if only in spirit. My mother remains fond of Jack and his wife to this day, living not far from them in the Palm Springs/Palm Desert area.

Mom went thorough one more series of professional changes just before meeting my dad.

From Betty to Ellie Mae to "Mom"

In short, my mother changed her name to Elinor Donahue and began a new chapter of her professional life.

Father Knows Best began as a radio program and made the transition into a television show in 1954. Except for the title lead of Jim Anderson, played by actor Robert Young, the parts for television were all recast. Elinor auditioned a few times for the role, having multiple callbacks, and at the age of sixteen she was cast in the role of the eldest child in the Anderson Family. The show ran for only one season on NBC beginning in 1954 before it was cancelled by the network. There was such an influx of letters from fans campaigning to save the program, that CBS picked it up and gave the show a better family viewing time slot. A few years later, NBC took it over again from CBS, and the show continued until the producers ended its original run in 1960.

During the run of *Father Knows Best,* my mom briefly married, through elopement, a studio sound technician named Richard Smith. It was certainly not widely known or welcomed that the woman playing America's teenager on the show was not only married, but pregnant during the run of the show. This development did not make the studio and production heads happy, and they did their best to keep the news quiet. She was now seen as a disappointment by most of the crew, cast, and producers. This was, after all, the 1950s version of the classic nuclear family. It's where on *I Love Lucy*, the married fictional Ricardos, played by the real-life married stars Desi Arnaz and Lucille Ball, when Lucy became pregnant in real life, and producers decided to use it in the show, they were unable to use the word "pregnant," and instead used the French word for pregnancy in the episode's title! So, what did the studio executives and producers of *Father Knows Best* do to hide that their teenage actress was actually pregnant?

The answer can best be seen in Season 3, Episode 29, "Betty the Track Star." There are a few episodes from this period where my mother is shown only in close-up shots or as the head peeking up and out over the shoulders of those who are standing in front of her. There is a scene where Betty is determined to accomplish two feats: run the relay race and accept the crown as Homecoming Queen. With the help of others, Betty runs the relay, wins, and then is quickly toweled off, dressed, and driven to the gymnasium where she steps up in time to receive her crown. This is a cute and typical storyline of the show, except for the fact that my mother was very pregnant with my older brother, Brian. If you look closely during this episode, you can occasionally see her "baby bump." In the relay race, she is fitted in a huge t-shirt for her running scenes as the high school track star, and you have never seen a waist so high on a prom dress, nor an outfit that billowed so below said high waist! By the time Brian came along, her marriage was essentially over, and the couple went their separate ways while both continuing to parent Brian until Mr. Smith's untimely death a few years later. Brian was later officially adopted by Harry and became the first of their four Ackerman boys.

Chapter 2

Mom and Dad Meet
(our early family life)

My parents married in 1961 after dating for over one year. They had first seen each other at the film studio and afterwards at many Television Academy events when my dad was the Academy's President. It was after my mother performed in a pilot for a series executive-produced by my dad, *Calling Miss Peters* (1960), when they officially began dating. It was during that production, that my mother remembered Dad had been in the room during the filming of an episode of another program a few years before, when he was in his role as Vice President of West Coast Programming for CBS. Additionally, when he served as President of the Academy of Television Arts and Sciences in Los Angeles, upon actress Jane Wyatt's suggestion, Dad brought Mom on to be a judge for a beauty contest related to the Emmy Awards show. Apparently, he knew that *Father Knows Best* was at an end, or at least it was a possibility, so he confidently cast my mother in *Calling Miss Peters*. The pilot, which did not get picked up, took place in a department store. My mother played someone who worked there and who was in a relationship with one of the managers, despite a "no dating between employees" policy. Before the days of home viewing equipment, my dad once surprised us and included this pilot in a screening in a private theater at The Beverly Hills Hotel for my mother, my brothers, and me. Though I do not recall much about the half-hour show, I do remember liking it, and loving the connection that it had to their relationship. Another connection is related to the fact that Hollywood is a small town.

In 1959, my mother was nominated for an Emmy Award by the Academy of Television Arts and Sciences. My dad served as the

President of the Academy at the same time. Alas, Mom did not win. the award was presented to actress Ann B. Davis for her role on *The Bob Cummings Show* (1955-1959). This lamentable event was only exacerbated by Ann B. Davis's later becoming "Alice" the family housekeeper on *The Brady Bunch* (1969-1974). In the continued awkwardness that the small television community sometimes was, my mother quietly watched *The Brady Bunch* along with me and my older brother on Friday nights, only occasionally mentioning that Miss Davis had beat her out for the Emmy. Still, my mother never spoke negatively about other actors, even when I laughed at something they did on screen.

Andy, She Hardly Knew Ye!

My mom finally completed a full, long series run with *Father Knows Best*. It was normal in the industry for cast members from one show to not get additional series work for a year or more. Moving against the trend, my mother immediately began work on the then-new program, The *Andy Griffith Show*, playing Ellie Walker, the town pharmacist. What is most remarkable about her time on the show is that even though she left before the conclusion of that first season, fans of the show still fondly remember her as a favorite character.

One of the memorable episodes from that season is shown frequently around Christmas. Andy, Ellie, and others decorate a tree in the town jail/sheriff's office as part of a Scrooge-like storyline. There my mother sings "Away in a Manger" with Andy as they decorate. Though I've heard versions of this story, my mother recently told me, in her words, "the true story."

> *"My call was at 7:00 PM at a small recording studio near Cahuenga Boulevard in Hollywood. Before I went my mother asked me why I was so nervous. 'You have sung this hundreds of times in Church. Just go and do it!'*
>
> *When I arrived, the producer Aaron Rubin (a very sweet and dear man), and a pianist were already there. We immediately*

got to work at the piano to find the right key that would suit Andy and my timid, shaking voice.

The studio itself was small and thickly carpeted. The piano was on a rise with two steps down to the actual recording area, with music stands and 'mikes' in booms. Sound techs were bustling about arranging the booms.

Andy said to me, 'Let's just sit down on these steps and we can run thru it 'til you're comfortable.' We sat and he began strumming his guitar a tech had handed him. He nodded to me and said, 'You just come in (sing) wherever you feel like it. Just nice and easy,' and he played the intro and we hummed along. He nodded his head at me and began the song.

When we finished, a voice from the sound booth that I hadn't even noticed called out, 'We got it! And it's great!'

It was recorded and we were finished, and after saying my stunned good-byes to everyone, I left. I looked at my watch and it wasn't even 7:30. I've come to believe that the "method" was planned before I arrived."

That was the take they used in the show, and if you listen carefully, you can hear how relaxed she sounds on the audio track!

Andy truly was a bit of a teaser behind the scenes. During her short stint on the series, my mother began dating my father, who was twenty-five years her senior. Even with both of them looking younger than their actual ages, the May-December romance was apparent. When he came by the set to visit her, she secretly hoped Andy wouldn't see, because if he did, he would, with his booming voice, announce with the proper inflection and teasing– "Hey, Ellie! Your BOY-friend is here! Thar he is, right over thar…your BOY-friend!" All in good fun but embarrassing still the same.

There are a few differing stories regarding her departure from *The Andy Griffith Show*. The truth in a simple statement-- my mother was exhausted. Not only did shows make more episodes in those days, but there were also many in-person press junkets to publicize the show. You couldn't just post a live story on Instagram and have word get out. Transitioning straight from *Father Knows Best* to *The Andy Griffith Show*, it soon became apparent that she needed a break. It wasn't just transitioning characters and acting styles, but she was leaving the stage of life as young adolescent and becoming a young, grown, and independent woman. She needed more time to develop the chemistry the producers wanted between her and Andy. Additionally, if you watch the first season, you will see it takes some time for Andy's character to settle into what it became; one where Don Knotts becomes the close partner instead of Miss Ellie. Any of these examples were reason enough for her to take a break from the never-ending Hollywood climb, but during that time she had also endured a marriage, divorce, childbearing, and loss of her ex-husband. It was now the fall of 1960, and little did she know that by April 1961 she would be married to Harry and their family would begin. She genuinely loved her craft and executives desired her for roles over the years, so while raising a family, she was able to keep one foot in the business, adding an impressive output of appearances onto her resume. It would be a decade and a half, though, before she had another opportunity to enjoy a series.

Home Life

My parents married on April 21, 1961, and exactly one year and one day later, was the birth of yours truly. Perhaps in a nod to their vocations, my appearance was in appropriate dramatic fashion. If this was a television script, it would be edited out as too unbelievable, but I promise I speak the truth.

Church affiliation was common in the early 1960s. My parents settled on joining the Episcopal Church after getting married because there was one in Beverly Hills, California, where a lot of families, in and out of show business, attended. In a congregation that included Hal Holbrook, some of the Roosevelts, Fred Astaire, Raymond Massey, and family friend, actress Mary Wickes, we found this parish was a great spiritual home for us. Though they initially desired to find a home church because of us children, faith reached deeper into Elinor.

My mother recalls the night before I was born as, *"Harry's and my first anniversary, when we went to All Saints Episcopal Church in the afternoon. It was a clear warm typical Southern California day, and it was [also] the day before Easter. My son Brian, age 5, was with us as he and I were going to be baptized into the church. I was pregnant with you and due to give birth in early May. During the ceremony, while standing in front of the congregation with Brian and several others, I felt a little tickle run up my back, and then a mild contraction."*

Making it through the baptism, they walked out with my mother certain this was it… that I was on my way. After rushing home, they phoned the doctor and left Brian with our grandmother, Doris (Nana), who was planning to stay with Brian while our parents went out to celebrate their anniversary. I ruined that though, however, and instead my parents rushed to St. Joseph's Medical Center in Burbank where at 1:31 AM on April 22nd, 1962 - Easter Sunday morning – Peter Kyran Ackerman, was born!

I did the Hollywood kid two-step right out of the gate! I rode my parents' figurative coattails to instant fame and was lifted into instant celebrity. Because they were at the peak of their careers at this time, I enjoyed birth announcements in both the *Daily Variety* and *Hollywood Reporter*. In showbiz terms, that was pretty much Sainthood! I was now well-ensconced in their birthday files where for about the first two decades of my life, I could look into the April 22 edition of either one of those publications and see my name listed among such real Hollywood luminaries as Glen Campbell and Dudley Moore.

By this time, and for a few years after my birth, my dad was fully engaged as the Executive Producer of many series. As previously mentioned, these included *Bewitched, The Flying Nun* (1967-1970), *Gidget* (1965-1966), *Leave it to Beaver (1957-1963)*, *Dennis the Menace (1959-1963)*, and *The Donna Reed Show (1958-1966)*.

My parents and older brother had moved into a house on Fryman Road, off of Laurel Canyon Boulevard, around the time they were married in 1960. It was a typical mid-century- modern home. Though there were larger houses down closer to Laurel Canyon from which Fryman broke off, ours was part of one side of the street that had been developed in the upper, flatter part of the long road. Today, it's very developed with many houses. I still can remember my older brother Brian bouncing on a pogo stick in the back yard while I was standing with Nana in the doorway of the house trying to wave down an ice cream truck. My very first memory ever was playing with a toy ice cream truck on a hallway floor. It made "jingle" sounds as it rolled, and as I played, I remember watching my mother in the doorway of a nearby room ironing. It seemed like such a normal family moment, one that happens regardless of what your parents do for a living. I always liked that.

As our family began to grow, with my arrival and my parents' desire to have more children, we moved to a magnificent home on Valley Meadow Road in Sherman Oaks. This is where most of the show business memories took place for me. The house was quite large, extending over the expansive property, yet retaining a homey look and feel. Even the pesky ivy which cascaded the hillside below the house looked manicured. As one drove up the winding driveway, he or she could see the wide house which hid how deep it went. To the right was the two-car garage and behind that sat the huge side porch and a large pool. The back of the house led up to hillsides where there stood the Ackerman boys' tree house. It's a tree house that holds a secret. It was here, as you will later read, where I told the son of a famous actress and director what really happened between his parents in their marriage. To the right of the driveway was a gift that I've cherished all my life. A tree. My tree. Today we live in a world that's fired up by our electronic devices, but when I was young, I remember going outside and standing and jumping as high as I could, trying to reach the closest branch above my head. When I finally was able to do so, I would begin standing lower in a rain ditch by the side, trying from that point until I was able to reach it there. I grew as it grew. That tree was everything to me. I pretended it was an airplane and flew to exotic places. It was a reading nook; it was my taste of heaven. Alas, the tree is no longer there today.

The interior of the house had been as comfortable and inviting as the outside, full of love and history. When you walked in the front door, there was a museum display case featuring President Abraham Lincoln's legal wallet and pocketknife which my father had purchased. To the left was the living room where Christmases were celebrated. To the right was the formal dining room which was used for special events. Moving deeper into the house brought you to the television and family room which connected to the small bar and very large kitchen with the smaller dining table where we boys regularly ate.

The living room was broad and homey. It was there I could sit and get lost either in my imagination or in the myriad of books that adorned the wall. My dad was very kind with lending me rare books and autographed items. I never gave a thought to some of the valuable and historical items that I casually took to school with me. I recognize my dad's permission as instilling trust in me, which I am grateful for. I might pass around in my class a check that aviator Charles A. Lindbergh signed to Ryan Airlines in partial payment for the instrumentation panel installed in The Spirit of St. Louis before it made the first transatlantic flight. I might have lugged, along with my schoolbooks, a first edition signed by Ernest Hemingway. When I developed a love of mysteries, I might have had with me one of the books by Raymond Chandler, inscribed "To Harry, Best Wishes, Raymond Chandler, La Jolla, CA." The latter my dad obtained when he was producing the radio show *The Adventures of Philip Marlowe* (1947-1950) and used to drive further south in California to run story ideas past the character's originator. Another favorite treasure in that room was the book signed to my dad by "Benedict Arnold Marx." Known more famously as Groucho, he inscribed in his book, *Groucho and Me*, an apology for making a last-minute deal with

NBC after he had solidified a handshake deal with my dad for CBS Television to produce *You Bet Your Life* (1950-1961). My dad only discovered the comedian's shrewd move when he read about it in the paper. As a forgiving man, he understood that business was business. Groucho readily admitted to him, with humor, that he was "Harry's personal traitor." The comedian signed the book affectionally as "Groucho 'Benedict Arnold' Marx."

Past the living room was a long hallway that led to the bedrooms of the house. There were three that kept alternating between my brothers and I as there slowly became more of us. This was home. This was our neighborhood. Some houses were bigger than others, but all in all, we were regular people. We had the Franks two doors down who had a child my age, Jonny, who I always played with, and the Kabus's house a few doors up where you could always see Mrs. Kabus looking at us through her kitchen window and her husband, Norm, tinkering away in his garage. I look back and remember those 1960s and early 1970s years very fondly. Yet, for a guy who has a life filled with stories, some in the home, some from the set, some from his own adventures in the business, life was anything but normal. This household was built by two very important individuals. Two people whose lives began long before I came along. Two people whose stories I am elated to tell you about.

One of my earliest memories was from the den of our Valley Meadow Road home where we lived from 1965 to 1977. I was about three years old, and I sat on my mother's lap while from not too far away she watched what was on the television screen and brought my attention to it. It must have been about 4:00 PM, and it was most likely KTLA Channel 5 because that was the channel that aired the show that proved to me-- my mom was on television. I don't recall the exact details, but I do know that it featured the character Betty Anderson walking through a door in glorious black and white and speaking to the rest of the cast. My mother leaned into my ear while pointing to the screen, saying, "Look Peter, there's mommy. That's mommy on the television!" As with many kids back in those days, we knew the "older" shows as black and white and our "new" ones were in color. I wondered if the world used to be in two-tone and was further intrigued when color came about. However, an idea that seemed completely realistic to me was that every mom appeared on television, right?

I was six years old. I can remember telling an old friend, Jonny Frank, that my mom was on KTLA Channel 5 at 4 O'clock. I then excitedly asked, "So, when is your mom on?" Jonny looked at me for the longest time before breaking the news to me that, "Peter, only your mom is on television, not everybody's mom is!" Talk about a growing moment. This started the string of questions with which I peppered my mother. "What do you do for a living?" "Why are only you on the television?" I might have been young, but let me tell you, when I learned you could have a job where you got to "pretend to be many different people" for a living, I was hooked.

It was also Jonny who told me one afternoon that my mom was on television, "with blonde hair!" We went into his living room and continued watching the noon movie that was being shown on a local station. Though I was not convinced, I remember thinking, "that blonde girl certainly looks like my mother." When I arrived home later that day, I went to where she was in the kitchen and I asked her, "Mom, did you ever have blonde hair?" She stopped what she was doing, turned, and said, "You saw *Girls Town*, didn't you?" It was more of a statement than a question. She told me the relentless casting story and how, unlike most actresses, she did everything she could to turn away from the cameras at every chance to hide her face! Later my grandmother provided me with the larger story surrounding my mom's casting in the movie. During a hiatus from *Father Knows Best*, her agent phoned her and explained, "Ellie, there is a low budget movie in the works, starring Mamie Van Doren, Harold Lloyd, Jr., Charlie Chaplin, Jr., Mel Torme and others. They want you to play Mamie's sister, who kills an attempted rapist, but Mamie takes the blame and goes to the women's prison over it." That was definitely not the kind of movie she dreamed of being in, but at this time in her career, she knew she couldn't afford to turn down roles. She absolutely did not want to do it and discussed the reasons why with her agent. He came to her rescue. He told her he'd go back to them and ask for so much money, they would have to turn him down. The phone rang an hour later and upon answering it, her agent informed her, "Well…I've got some good news and some bad news." It was after this moment she appeared in the film *Girls Town* (1959). It's the only movie where she remains almost unrecognizable, almost. Still, *Girls Town* remains a cult classic to this day, and I have to admit, it's fun to watch when it comes on television. Still, the blonde femme fatale was hidden enough that it did not impact her continuing on the show she was working on at the time especially when she quickly returned to the brunette that she was.

Her natural look was not only needed for *Father Knows Best*, but also serves as a metaphor to how we boys in the Ackerman household were raised.

The Family

My parents were very grounded. They never got lost in their fame. I wasn't raised as an elitist, which happens often in Hollywood. People who looked differently than me, who worked certain jobs, who were in lower economic circumstances, weren't treated any differently by my parents. I learned respect by their example. I'm extremely grateful when I meet industry people who have heard of my family and remember me as, "not the typical Hollywood kid!" At the same time, though, I recognize that my childhood was very atypical. The Ackerman household was definitely unlike the homes of many of my friends, but at its core, it was home.

Though I focus on my adventures and what it was like growing up with my parents, I also want to elaborate on some of the family members I have mentioned throughout. My older brother, Brian, was six years older than I and was the son of our mom and her first husband. After she and my dad married, and because of the death of

Brian's birth father, my older brother was legally adopted by our dad and officially became an Ackerman.

Brian always felt called to water. He swam on the high school team and from a young age fell in love with sailing. After college, Brian became a chef and baker, but the sea always called to him. He has been in Northern California for decades, but for a while lived on a houseboat once owned by author Earle Stanley Gardner, who wrote the *Perry Mason* novels, which impressed me as the avid fiction reader I am. Brian is currently a ship's captain and works out of the Monterey Bay area of California. Married to Melissa, they are parents to Maddy, who is currently following in her grandmother Elinor's footsteps.

My younger brother, James, arrived on the scene three years after me and is an amazing individual. Though I feel that I resemble the best qualities of our mother, James exhibits those same assets, but from our father. After high school, James went on an adventurous search for what life held for him. Ever a fan of the film *PT 109* (1963), he first sought direction by serving in the Coast Guard. Following that he entered into various vocations, eventually settling as the President and CEO of Prison Fellowship. The organization helps to bring Christian faith to prisoners and care for their families while they are incarcerated. His was among the many whose efforts behind the scenes led to a popular bi-partisan bill to pass Congress at a time when the body did not usually work together. James is a "what-you-see-is-what-you-get" kind of person. He is intelligent, thoughtful, and a good conversationalist. He is a person of deep Christian faith who recognizes when doors open to him, and he walks through them. In the mid-1980s, he married his dear Martha, and they are parents to Holden and Lily.

Then there's my "baby" brother, Chris. There was difficulty around his birth, and I'm not sure how much I was supposed to know back then, but I remember our mother being pregnant and having been around for James' birth, I thought nothing of it. What I know now is that Chris was born prematurely, underweight, and struggling. My parents kept six-year-old me oblivious to this reality, but my school knew, most likely in the case they needed to console me while my mother and new brother were still in the hospital. It was at Burmar Elementary School in 1968 I lined up with my schoolmates to get onto the proper bus to drop me off at home. As I stood in line, one of the teachers came over to me and in a pastoral tone, she attempted to lift my spirits. The problem is, I didn't understand the extra concern over my mother's pregnancy or that my spirits needed lifting! The principal, who also knew of the situation, interjected herself into the conversation and attempted to bring the comments from the teacher into context for me, concluding with, "Don't worry, everything will be alright." Although I was clueless, she thankfully was certainly right.

Following Chris' birth, after his arrival home, I vividly remember the first time I got to see him. My parents escorted me over to his bedroom, where I peeked into the crib, and there before me was the tiniest baby person that I still to this day had ever laid eyes on. He was so very small, but thankfully has grown into a vibrant and healthy man. His spirit can hardly be contained within his frame. If I passed anything along to him in our lives it was my love of live concerts. He still collects souvenirs from shows that he and/or I attend and has kept all the others from back in the day. He has the business sense of our brother James, the spirit of adventure lived out by Brian, and the performing bug permanently contained within yours truly. Besides working in the field of public transportation, one can find him at motorcycle racing events throughout California in his other guise; an announcer named, "Crazy Chris!" At home, Chris is married to Leanne, and they are also parents to two great and equally talented young adults, Liam and Aubrey. His and Leeann's wedding was significant to me, as it was the last time all four Ackerman boys, plus our half-brother Steve, were together at one event.

And speaking of my half-siblings, Steve and Susan, from my dad's first marriage were teens by the time I became a part of the Ackerman household. At the time of my birth, they were living with their mother in nearby Beverly Hills. As I grew older, and because I only saw them on weekends when they would visit, I began to question who they were and why we only saw them the way we did. When I was about six, I finally asked Steve, a little aggressively I admit, "Why are you here all the time?" With his Groucho Marx-esque humor and a deep hearty laugh, that was both unique to him and reminiscent of our dad, Steve looked at me like I had just landed from space and exclaimed, "I'm your brother!" For me, it was a delightful surprise to know I had other siblings.

Steve married Francine (Frannie) Selkirk, a woman I admire to this day. No longer married to my half-brother, Francine and Steve also added to my uncle bonafides, first by giving birth to Dailey, and later adopting a child, Jessica, from another couple in the neighborhood after those parents tragically died. I love those kids, now adults as well.

My half-sister Susan was no slouch in the humor department either. Up until she died in 2020, she swore that the Beach Boys' song *Fun, Fun, Fun* (1964), about the young girl taking "daddy's car" on a joyride, was about her. Susan was classmates and best friends with Candice Bergen when they attended Marlborough Girls Academy in Beverly Hills, California. Friends, until Susan was asked to leave the school, after getting caught in some shenanigans. Many years later, when I worked in production on a television commercial with Candice, the actress reminisced about their time together. Candice reminded me a lot of my sister and so I'm unclear whether I imagined the conversation or if she implied that she was involved in some of the shenanigans that ultimately got Susan "excused" early from the school. Susan had a wicked sense of humor, and plus she could burp on cue, and that was just awesome. Not just a quick "belch," but one of those that you could talk a whole sentence through. Apparently when working as a flight attendant, Susan used to win dares by making flight announcements that way. Yes, we in the Ackerman clan were certainly a classy bunch! Though they were primarily raised by Mary, I'm glad and thankful that these two were a part of my life growing up. And because of them, more relatives came.

Susan, with later husband Rich, had more of an aunt and uncle vibe, something that remained up until their passings. My earliest memory of Rich and Susan was one of their favorites, when I served as ring bearer at their wedding. I may have become hooked on making people laugh when the pillow, which I was holding with white gloves, kept slipping from my hands and falling on the floor or the church. Susan and I were definitely from the same tribe. She loved to laugh and knew how to tell a story. She and Rich made me an uncle with first Brett, and next with twins Carrie and Kellie. I was under 10 years old and an uncle!

Finally, there was my grandmother, who lived nearby or with us, Nana. She and I had a special relationship, and it was because of her I learned to identify as the "middle child" in the midst of four children. My younger brothers by three years each, James and Chris, bonded together as boyhood pals, while my older by six years brother Brian was often doing his own things, while sometimes allowing me to tag along. Being that I was somewhat shy at the time, and a bit of a loner, Nana became the family member whom I gravitated towards.

At Nana's apartment, I could do anything. I would watch television or read comic books, the latter eventually evolving into paperback novels. As a young teenager, after discovering I enjoyed musicals, I found a whole new world when I was introduced to Nana's record collection. It's there, years before I ever saw the movie, that I listened to the soundtrack of the Danny Kaye biopic of cornet player Red Nichols, *The Five Pennies* (1959), which enticed me to take trumpet lessons for a while.

Nana was also a fun storyteller. Whether telling me about what went on when she babysat the boy next door, stories around my mother's early career, or what happened when she was out shopping, she had a knack for recounting events and mining from them interesting, funny, and overall delightful anecdotes. She saw a lot because she did not hurry. She refused to learn how to drive, and that forced her to walk everywhere. For longer excursions, she took public transportation, and it was there that I learned a tremendous life lesson.

Returning from shopping in Los Angeles, Nana and I rode the bus from downtown back to her home in the Sherman Oaks area of the San Fernando Valley. It was around 1968, and I was six years old. I sat in the aisle seat of our row and looked around at the other passengers. They were all women, adorned in ladies-out-shopping attire, as was common in those days. They all seemed to have well-coiffed white cotton-like hair, pearls around their necks and wrists, and dressed as one might be for a religious service. Every double set of seats on the bus had at least one person in the row, but there was still plenty of room for other passengers. However, that changed after the bus stopped to pick up a new passenger. There was some uncomfortable activity among the women around Nana and me, one of them saying, "Don't let her sit." The women began maneuvering around. One took her shopping bags and put them on the aisle seat next to her and turned towards the window, leaving her broad back and bags as a signal that no interaction was to take place. Another shopper scooted herself to her aisle seat and put her bags onto the window seat beside her. I might not have known what was going on if not for Nana. A Black woman stepped onto the bus. As she did, I realized it was because of her that the shoppers shifted the way they did. As our new passenger made her way down the aisle, she began asking if she could sit in the seat that was next to each passenger. She was met either with silence or mumbled "harrumph" responses. Nana said out loud, as much to me as to the inconsiderate racist white "ladies" in question, "I cannot believe it. They aren't going to let her sit!" Those words and the actions, or rather inactions, before me became a front row ticket to me viewing racism plain as day. Nana grabbed me and directed me to sit on her lap. I resisted, claiming that I was a "big boy," and began to squirm, but her demand was so out of character that I acquiesced quickly. Nana invited the woman to sit next to us.

These many years later, I can recall looking at this woman who then sat next to me. Unlike Nana, she wasn't surprised by the rudeness at hand, and perhaps she took it in stride. She looked down at me and smiled. Then she looked at Nana and thanked her. As the woman's gaze returned to me, she said "Your grandmother is someone special." That day, I saw what truly goes into a choice. I could choose to be like the shopping ladies, who now turned their ire upon Nana, saying, "Can you believe she let her *sit* next them?" Or, I could understand that sometimes in life to do the right thing, we have to be ready to be uncomfortable in the process. Nana didn't have a lot of money, we didn't have large billowing shopping bags like other riders on that bus, but through Nana's action, and the woman's appreciation, I understood that dignity through love and service was a special place, a holy one, on which we are called to dare stand, or in this case, sit upon.

Nana died in her late 90s. She still lived in her apartment and passed on quietly while reading a book. Though she had met my son, her great-grandson, she had not yet met her newly born great-granddaughter. My only hope, as a parent, is that I offer the way of life, through the choices I make in the face of adversity, that Nana taught me. Home, at its core, is about family, and with the family members described, I grew up in a home that was connected, through my parents, to the Classic Television world.

Chapter 3

Home, Hollywood, and Its Perks

My first memories were of how our home, with two parents associated with Classic Television, functioned and looked similar to many homes at the time, except for the fact that occasionally my mother was a working one: a rare role in the more traditional domiciles in the neighborhood. After we boys enjoyed a breakfast of cereal, juice, and a vitamin, Dad would come out of the bedroom and head to work. In the evening, he would return, very much like the dad on a sitcom. On days my mother didn't work, her schedule consisted of shuttling her kids, and others, to scouting, school events, church functions, and the grocery store. My life seemed normal, but looking back, I realize that it was not.

Did you ever have a Rams football player toss the pigskin to you in your driveway? I did. Mike Henry was a former pro football player, an actor, and a friend of my parents. Mike came over to the house a few times, and on one occasion my dad brought out a football and Mike put me through my paces. He played many roles over time, including Junior the sheriff in the *Smokey and the Bandit* movies (1977, 1980, 1983). My favorite role for him was in the three films where he played a more James Bond-like Tarzan. So, forget football-- I was hanging out with Tarzan, and for me that was a big deal!

In the evenings, my parents ate dinner later than we boys and would often have guests. On those nights, we were invited to come out in our pajamas, robes, and slippers and meet their friends before saying goodnight. Whether it was Steve Allen and his wife Jayne Meadows, or a television writer, director, or producer, that experience was just part of a sometimes-nightly routine in our house.

Better were our parties. When we first settled in our home, my mother was still a highly sought-after actress and Dad was extremely successful with his slate of shows, including *Hazel*, *Dennis the Menace*, *Bewitched*, and more. Occasionally, a real "Hollywood" party would take place right in our home. I have always enjoyed watching and observing people. When I was younger, I was also very shy, so it was in my nature at large gatherings to quietly drift around and observe. It was at a huge affair in my parents' home when I did just that and came upon a group of people in the family room. They were enraptured with whomever was speaking; for a moment he looked at me, this little child in his Sunday best, in the midst of their huddle, but then moved on back to his conversation. I was soon forgotten, but I remained, and I listened. With great authority, the speaker continued; "As I was saying, my new book is about the time I spent exploring Africa with actual pygmies…" As he continued, I thought to myself, "Wow, a real African explorer!" As I gazed around the room, I just felt like I was among "my people," the colleagues of my parents. My favorite celebrity friend, Mike "Tarzan" Henry, was present. Not too far away was Sally Field. Everyone just stood in conversation while being served food and drinks, and it always felt a little like heaven to me. Or at least show biz heaven. It was at that moment, while the African Explorer continued his anecdotes, that I said to myself, "I want to be a part of this experience; these people." In the most declarative thought in my life, I decided how I was going to do accomplish that. I said to myself, "I am going to be an actor."

I realize now that I probably stumbled into the same role held by my mother and not my father, because in all honesty, I never really understood for many years what he actually did. When I went to the studio with him, he would drop me onto a set, tell someone to watch out for me, and then leave to head to his office for meetings. Though I later began to understand what he did by on set observation, and later in life driving him around, suffice it to say, at the time we lived in the Valley Meadow Road home, all I knew was that they were busy. And if the parents are busy, and the one grandparent does not drive, what to do when I had to go to a dentist appointment right after school? Send the limo!

Along with *Bewitched* director, Bill Asher, and his wife Elizabeth Montgomery, whom you will hear more about later, my parents shared the cost for the services of Joe Fagan and his stretch limo. It was nice, long, shiny, and black, complete with a partition one could control from the back to block the front seat driver from hearing your conversations. Joe was the go-to guy when an extra vehicle and driver were needed. Even though other children from show business families attended my school, St. Cyril's, no one was so ostentatious to be picked up at 2:40 PM (my favorite time of day because that was when school let out) in a limo, let alone in a limo to be taken to the dentist!

I remember how cool and down-to-earth Joe was. Even though he would joke with us kids, like any good chauffeur, he was waiting outside of the vehicle as I walked out from school. With all schoolmate eyes on me, I stopped and looked up at Joe and asked, "Joe, is it okay if I sit with you in the front?" He replied with, "Sure, just don't tell your family." Of course, I had experienced the fun of sitting in the back, "the important seats" as they're known. I distinctly remember my classmates turning back to their previous engagements after I climbed into the front seat, almost as if saying, "Oh, it's no one important, because he didn't get in the back." As far as they knew, I was a chauffeur's boy, and that was just fine for me. Joe was of Irish heritage, and a great storyteller. Over the years, I grew to know him well, after hearing tales of his concerts, athletic events, and more. The combination of being an affable, friendly fellow who wore a chauffeur's uniform and had a limo nearby, gave him the ability to talk his way into almost any event, whether it was a Lakers game or an Elton John concert. He was a true character and a lovely man.

As embarrassed as I was to be picked up by a limo, there were the one-of-a-kind perks that I never took for granted. Who else could get picked up by their parents after school and head on a drive along the 405 Freeway, get off at the Goodyear Blimp hangar, and actually ride the blimp? I did…twice! At the time, people could apply to ride the dirigible, and that's just what my parents did. We had to show up to the field in Los Angeles on a certain day and time. From there, we were escorted into the basket of the blimp, which sat passengers similarly to how they do in an airplane (but with no restroom). The pilots up front then powered up the extremely loud engines while the grounds crew let go of the anchoring ropes. Once we were at an elevation and location that the pilots were comfortable with, the engines were shut off and we floated. It was amazing. I could see my hometown in ways I never had before. The best part was the return. In order to get close to the landing area, the blimp had to do a nosedive right over one of the holes at a nearby golf course. On one trip, our pilot took delight in the fist-shaking reaction he received from one of the golfers below. What did *you* do after school?

About this time, my love of show business, along with my visits to the sets and helping my mother with her lines, made me a self-studied student of the Classic Television genre. I began watching programs critically. What made me laugh? Would I do so if the laugh track had not prompted me to do so? I am not sure when this manner of observing television settled into me, but I have it to this day. In fact, I have to see any movie twice before deciding if I like it. During the first viewing, my mind wanders into the technical realm. After a second look I can actually appreciate the story on its merits. Recently, it took me about six viewings of the fabulous movie *Once Upon a Time in…Hollywood* (2019) to determine if I liked the film's story structure. I did.

While my television viewing expertise grew, my school grades faltered. My father, a man who felt that education was a valuable asset and one had to think ahead and do well now to be better positioned in the future, was not happy with my scores. He was right. At best I was an unmotivated C-student. Though my teachers at St. Cyril's Catholic School in Encino, like Sister Carmel, did their best, it was determined that harsh measures were needed to get me focused on my schoolwork. For a couple of years, except for special occasions, I was no longer allowed to watch television.

As a young grade schooler, I did understand the denial of television viewing. I felt that school was really teaching me traits that I did not need to know. Why do I need to know how to do fractions or diagram a sentence? But, as time passed, and I turned to reading books, and my grades eventually improved. Regardless of if I watched television or not, I was a walking expert on what was to air during the week. I could recite what show was on what channel and when, as well as the description of the specific episode that was aired.

TV Guide of the 1970s was essentially my bible. I believe that *TV Guide* was then *the* primary way to figure out what was on and when. The magazine arrived in the mail on Thursdays, and I went searching for it the moment I came home from school. In preparation for the following weeks' worth of programs, I devoured the information from the magazine. I knew which *Thin Man* movie was on at 3:00 AM, and if *The Six Million Dollar Man* (1974-1978) was a repeat or not. The bonus treat was the annual *Fall Preview Guide*. From that I knew which shows were premiering, what specials were in production, and what movies were going to be televised. On top of that were the TV/film industry papers, also known as the "trades:" *The Hollywood Reporter* and *Daily Variety*. Perusing those, I learned what films were in development, and determined where the industry was putting its focus. Even those films in the earliest levels of production sometimes had beautiful posters created, inviting an imaginative lad like me to vision the yet-unmade movie. These magazines about the industry were all great springboards for a boy with an active imagination. Sadly, I never got to use my imagined talents in the industry. I wonder what would have happened, if my dad had actually encouraged my encyclopedic knowledge of show business at the time. Alas, he, instead, gave me the same lecture that a classic TV dad would to his son: "Peter, if you would only apply yourself to your studies like you do the *TV Guide*, you could really make something of yourself!"

Maybe, but I loved entertainment, and living at home with a dad who loved old movies only led me further into enjoying the entertainment industry. As a film aficionado, my dad regularly took me to see films presented by the Los Angeles County Museum of Art. Chaplain, Stewart, Wayne, Brando. The films of John Ford. These are just some of the film masters I was exposed to, and whose work I was grateful to have been able to study from such an early age.

The museum usually had a summer series, curated by a man named Ron Haver, where they would show at least two films in the course of one evening. In the days before DVDs, it was here I would be exposed to the bonus material or narrated tracks that provided the history and background of the movie. I was able to see the circumstances surrounding certain productions and learn extensive behind-the-scenes trivia. On a double feature night, however, we rarely stayed for the second film, due to school, church, or Dad's schedule the next day. Mr. Haver would always speak about the movie right before rolling, and afterwards as the opening credits played, we would take that opportunity to sneak out. We'd pass by Mr. Haver and his disapproving scowl as we walk-of-shamed our way out of the museum. Always felt a little guilty about that.

It was in that same theater where my older brother, Brian, took his girlfriend and me to a showing of a 1936 movie called *Things to Come*. Based on an H.G. Wells story, the plot told of a futuristic society. Actor Raymond Massey starred in the film, and I was as engaged with the story as with any good black and white film until I saw something that took me back. Massey's character ages throughout the production until he is an old man with white hair. Darn it if he did not look exactly like the white-haired old man, albeit with two canes, who sat behind me in church every Sunday. The man with whom I shook hands whenever we exchanged, what is called The Peace, in the middle of the service.

On the way home I remarked to Brian and his girlfriend, who also were regular attendees to All Saints Episcopal Church in

Beverly Hills, how the old man we sat near in church looked just like the old man in the movie. They just laughed and told me the reason that the actor looked familiar was that the actor in the movie, Raymond Massey, was the very same older fellow who sat behind us in church!

Yes, even at the Ackerman family church, show business held its draw. Besides those people already mentioned and Mr. Massey, there were other actors and entertainers who worshipped there, Mary Wickes, Hal Holbrook, Dixie Carter, and Randolph Scott. My favorite though, was Fred Astaire, who used to leave the worship service early. Sometimes, when I was a little older, I would sit outside the side doors he exited from, and accept his good morning nod, as he almost danced down the steps, and began his walk-strut home.

As memory serves, no matter how "normal" we were as a family, "Hollywood" often appeared in surprising ways. There was the time I arrived home from school only to discover a mountain full of toys piled upon our side porch! This once-in-my-lifetime occurrence happened thanks, in part, to Groucho Marx. Groucho was a member of the Hillcrest Country Club, along with my godfather, director Eddie Buzzell, and his best friend, one cigar-smoking George Burns. My parents would run into some or all of these fellows over the course of house parties and elaborate dinners. On one occasion my mother was seated at the table with a certain film producer, who will remain anonymous. Over the course of the meal, and perhaps many, many cocktails, this producer became ever more insulting towards my mother.

Unknown to anyone at the table, this producer recently requested his female assistant to contact a specific actress, telling her it was "that woman who plays Betty Anderson on that television show." Of course, the producer meant Elinor Donahue, but the assistant instead reached out to another actress who was currently co-starring in *Peyton Place* as a character also named Betty Anderson. After she, directly or via an agent, turned down the producer in a way that seemed cruel and unkind, this man now held a grudge. The only problem was he believed this response came from Elinor Donahue, and he was letting her have it at dinner. Finally, as things were starting to become uncomfortable, Groucho spoke up and told the producer to cut it out. Though my mother can't remember exactly what the comedian said, she described it as authoritative, funny, and biting. With a head full of steam, the next morning the producer went to gather the evidence to prove to Groucho that this "Betty Anderson" was not worth defending. It was then he discovered the mix-up and learned that it was not Elinor who turned down a part in one of his films! He apologized in an amazing and profuse manner.

My brothers and I arrived home from school one day to find our side porch stacked with a pyramid of toys, puzzles, and games. This producer, knowing she had a family, seemed to take it upon himself to purchase one of everything from a toy store, which I was not about to complain about. My parents allowed us each to choose one box to keep for ourselves, and the rest went to charity. I chose a magic set, and little did I know this would begin my climb to later serious amateur magician status. Becoming a Magician Member of the Academy of Magical Arts is something I can proudly attribute to the actions of both a famous Hollywood producer and Groucho Marx! My home experience included a lot of actors, but I spent plenty of time seeing them in their natural working habitat, the film studios. Like a first love, I remember my first trip to a studio lot.

My First Film Studio Adventure with the Caped Crusader

I first noticed how connected my senses were to film studios when, as a boy, I walked into a strip mall next to my school to buy a snack, before heading home, and walked past a building extension that had recently been erected. The smell of fresh cut wood transported me instantly back to the film studios I went to with my parents. Because construction crews are always building sets, on and off soundstages, that wood scent is ever-present, as it was the first time I went to a studio.

My very first trip onto a film studio set was not the show my dad executive produced, *Bewitched*, but another production I have to admit I loved even more. One morning, with my dad driving our car, my mother in the front passenger seat, and my older brother Brian and I in the back, we headed to the studio sets of *Batman* and *The Monkees*. The family had a basic record player in our den and being that he was an executive at Columbia Television in the department known as Screen Gems, my dad had free access to record albums. I remember the first rock-and-roll record I listened to at four-years-old was the (still favorite of mine) *Headquarters* by The Monkees. Later, I would listen to *The Partridge Family* records, and even one with songs sung by Sally Field on *The Flying Nun*, but eventually I would graduate to more mainstream groups like The Beatles and would later go on to work in music video productions. On the day of my first visit to a set, headed to see Batman and the Monkees, as we drove up to the guard gate, even I knew something wasn't right. It was my mother who said, "Oh dear, what happened there?" As I looked, I saw the long "arm" that would go up to allow cars to pass had been broken off with some force. It leaned up against a fence, to the right of our vehicle. I still remember the pale wooden splinters sticking out from where the break occurred. My dad rolled down his window and the guard who was standing outside of the shack began to wave us through, but my dad stopped the car and asked what happened. In a curmudgeonly voice that would have made Ebenezer Scrooge proud, he responded, "Oh it was that *Peter* kid, from *The Monkees*." He was spitting mad when he said the name; one that I was so familiar with. He continued on, saying, "He came to the gate and before I could raise it, he just drove through it." My father responded, "Oh, I am so sorry to hear that." The studio guard shrugged his epaulet covered security jacket shoulders, "Ah, what are you going to do with these kids these days?" As he waved us through, I will never forget the look we all received from my mother. Though she looked at my dad as if to bore her point home, her words were just as pointedly delivered to us riding in the back. "I don't think we will be visiting *that* set today!" We did not, as it turned out, and what happened next made me pretty much forget about visiting *The Monkees* set. (Fortunately, years later, while I was working in television, I had the opportunity to hang out backstage after one of their concerts. And even though I stood near Peter Tork and nodded a "hello" to which he smiled back. I never shared with him his part in my own past.).

Oh, but where did I go that day? The set of the greatest television series ever: *Batman.* Though neither of my parents had any professional connection to the Adam West series, we still had another tie. Bill Dozier, the Executive Producer and narrator of the series, had been a protégé of my dad's and had worked under him in the past. As a professional favor, Mr. Dozier invited my family and me to visit the set of my favorite show. The experience did not disappoint!

As we entered the soundstage and navigated our way around unused lights and over thick wound cables that were on the floor, we headed towards the sound of activity from which light and heat emanated and my heartbeat rose with anticipation. There was also the smell that will take me right back to that moment and every moment that I visit a stage set, the scent of sawdust.

I heard it before I saw it, but we got in range just in time. We were well back from the camera that was filming the action but positioned perfectly to see the two superheroes in action as they were being tortured by the Catwoman. They were filming the episode, "Hot Off the Griddle" for the second season of the series. When I watch this particular scene today, I remember the dialogue clearly as Batman teaches Robin how to jump from foot to foot so as to prevent them from burning on the giant hot floor they were placed on. From the top of the set, where she looked down and taunted my heroes, was Julie Newmar.

Walking around between shots, my brother Brian and I explored the area to find where we could best watch the filming. We stumbled on the interior set of "Stately Wayne Manor." Brian pointed at the bust of Shakespeare, head opened, already revealing the button that would open up the bookcase entrance to the poles to the Batcave. Sure enough, right where it was supposed to be, was the sliding bookcase already well ajar. I walked over and looked downward. I expected and wanted to see the Batcave, with the Batmobile and the Bat-computer with flickering, flashing lights, but none of that was down below. Instead, the drop went about six feet or so, and ended with pillows to gently catch the fall of the actors as they went downward. Although disappointment seemed inevitable, I found myself instead thinking that television was storytelling, and what looked real was just pretend. Seeing and growing up around the innerworkings, I knew people put it all together to make the glamorous show. I loved that idea. I wanted to be a part of that process, of that magic. In that moment, I became determined to work, at least part of my life, in show business.

Bill Dozier and my parents returned to us, and with them was actor Adam West (what?!), who had now taken off the hero's cowl and put a white terrycloth robe around himself. A studio photographer was on set, and he asked us to gather together for a photo, which I still own and cherish to this day. Everyone's smiling, and I am in my father's arms again looking directly into the lens, and my eyes look wider than I ever remember them being. I guess meeting one's hero in real life had me speechless. The rest of the day is a blur, but it doesn't matter. That was the day that I met Batman.

Years later, I ended up at a signing with Adam West where he signed the photo from that day for me. If you have never met Adam West in real life, you have missed a true treat. Many actors draw upon their own experiences for their characters, and Mr. West was no different. While examining the photo I placed before him, he asked in his sonorous voice, "I know these people. Who are your parents?" After telling him about Harry and Elinor, he began recalling their work, memories, and character. He signed the photo, "To my old pal, Peter." What could be better than that? I have to say that with as many extraordinary memories I get to carry with me, that takes the cake by far.

There were also opportunities not taken. One example happened in the mid-1970s. I became of fan of the legendary ventriloquist Edgar Bergen, father of actress (and my half-sister's high school pal) Candice. I feel so fortunate that when Mr. Bergen came out of retirement to perform again, I got to see him live. In Century City, he was the featured performer at a two-night tribute to Vaudeville at the Shubert Theatre. My parents took me to opening night and that was one of the few times I faced the paparazzi. I will never forget watching my mother instantly know how to address all of the cameras, looking left to right, slowly, gazing for a few moments into each lens. It was one of those times when you just become enamored watching a person you know so well take on the demeanor of who they needed to be in that moment. "This way Elinor! Who's this with you, Elinor? Elinor, over here!"

Though I doubt they cared, she made sure to identify me to them, and not long after a photo of her and me appeared in gossip columnist Rona Barrett's magazine. While the highlight of that night was watching Edgar Bergen and Charlie McCarthy, I still smile when I see those glamorous photos of me and my mom. On our drive home that evening, my dad told me of his friendship with Mr. Bergen and how they corresponded regularly. (I still own one of the letters he sent my father, and I cherish it). My mother suggested that we contact him and see if he would give me a lesson in ventriloquism. What an opportunity! Alas, I was in a stubborn, sullen teenager phase and told them I would think about it. I never brought it up again, and the masterful performer sadly died the next year, so it wasn't meant for me to pursue ventriloquism as a career. Regardless, life in front of and behind the camera was always where I wanted to be. The set of Bewitched became the first regular soundstage I would often visit.

My Early Days on the Bewitched Set

I already mentioned the presence of Bill Asher and Elizabeth Montgomery in our lives. The family connection extended to others on the *Bewitched* set. The Dick Sargent years on *Bewitched* coincided with my visits to the set. The first time I remember being on the stage was truly magical... That day, my dad walked me around and showed me some of the technical aspects of a soundstage. As they filmed a sequence having to do with a "Witches' Convention" there were many actors and extras dressed in various witch-and-warlock-wear meandering around set. There was dry ice pumped in to look like smoke. My dad really picked a good day to take me! There was also a camera on a tall crane, and after my dad introduced me to the man in charge, the man turned to my dad and asked, "Harry, is it alright if I take him up?" My father replied, "If he wants to!" The man then turned to me and said "How about it, Peter? You sit right here on the chair where the director sits, we'll strap you in, I'll ride where the cameraman sits, and you can see how we film these shows. How about it?" Thankfully, I replied "yes," and after getting buckled in we went up, and up, and up, and up. As we continued to climb, I looked down upon the extras in the scene, and then got to look through the lens which brought them much closer. I remember how cool it was to be looking through the lens of an actual film camera while being lifted up, and soon we glided back down. It was and remains to this day an amazing memory. It was one of many of that wonderful day, on that marvelous soundstage.

It was then that I met the great Agnes Moorehead. Even though she was covered in the frightening makeup of Endora, and though she sounded much the same, there was a warmth and kindness that emanated from her. She stooped down and engaged me in a brief conversation. She was wonderfully nice. My only wish is that my present self, a fan of the work of Orson Welles, could go back and appreciate the time I met and spoke with one of Welles' Mercury Players!

When our conversation concluded as she was called onto the set, I looked for my dad who had drifted away and was now conferring with some others nearby. As I began my walk to him, this pretty, sassy brunette woman approached me. She beamed excitedly and came right up to me, bending her knees as she lowered to my level. "And who might you be?" she asked. After telling her my name, she brought herself conspiratorially close to my face and asked, "Oh, what do you think of the other actors, like Elizabeth Montgomery, is she nice?" In figuring out how to answer, I suddenly heard a voice callout from set, probably the director's and quite possibly my unofficial uncle Bill Asher, "Where's Serena!?" The woman immediately straightened up and quickly said, "I have to go, honey. It was nice meeting you," and then she strutted onto the set, apologizing to everyone, "Sorry! I just had to 'tinkle'!"

This actress, credited on the series as Pandora Spocks, was actually Liz Montgomery in a special wig and makeup. I am completely truthful when I say I had NO idea. She 100% convinced me she was someone else. In a further nod to her enjoying having an alter ego, in my dad's office there used to hang two large, framed photos which were personally signed to him. One from Liz and one from "Serena!"

It was bad enough that I was fooled on the set, but for too many years I swore up and down to friends at school that they were two different actresses, as I had met them both.

Though I only met "Serena" once, there were certainly many other fun visits to the *Bewitched* set. If I went to the studio with my dad, going to that soundstage was like popping over to visit a friend who lived next door. It was a good, welcoming, and fun place to visit. There was an atmosphere on the sets of my dad's shows, especially among the crew, that was welcoming and collegial. Everyone was there to do a job. Later in my life when I began working on various shows, I could often see throughout the production and talent an exercising of egos. This just wasn't as prevalent in the days of classic TV.

I also met Dick Sargent, who played Darrin, the husband of Montgomery's Samantha, on the final years of the series. Dick was a wonderfully nice fellow. Because of my age, I never had the opportunity to meet the first actor who portrayed Darrin, Dick York.

Later in life, through a conversation with my dad, I learned how they segued from one actor to the other. Today we might see Bewitched on more than one cable television network, and we miss the flow. It is jarring for first time viewers to see one Darrin actor, and suddenly the other. But in the early days of television, when episodes were shown for the first time, there was an easier way to make the transition.

The first aspect to the change that helped was the unfortunate reason that they had to do it; Dick York was not well. A back injury led to pain medication, and later to an addiction. The actor began missing his days for filming. Sometimes they filmed around him, but it became easier to do quick rewrites taking the character out of the scene altogether. When Mr. York left the show, they filmed a series of episodes where Darrin was never seen. He was kept "present" by Samantha talking to him on the phone, though the actor was never seen or heard.

Working with the network, my dad came up with a plan. They would save these Darrin-less episodes for the summer when most programs were repeating their episodes from earlier in the year. This move of offering new episodes of Bewitched in the summer kept up viewership, and allowed over the course of many weeks for people to forget about what Darrin looked and sounded like. These new episodes led directly towards the new season, and when Dick Sargent suddenly appeared as the husband, it was different, but not as jarring, as my dad helped the audience to segue from one performer to the next. Though I regret not meeting Dick York, I am so happy for the people who I got to meet from the show.

A TV show executive produced by Harry felt like a family. I believe to this day the core reason is that my father was one who respected all. Just as I have shared before from our home life, Dad never accepted the notion of acting superior because of the opportunities we could enjoy. In the production world overseen by my dad, everyone was of equal worth. How many times I have read this or heard this about him? I still appreciate it every time I do.

As *Bewitched* progressed, I was now regularly watching what we would refer to today as Classic Television. Many actors who worked on one show might guest on another, so I was always seeing familiar faces through the day. While Dad visited with Bert Convy who was on Bewitched playing the revolutionary, Paul Revere, I wandered and happened upon another guest actor sitting in a guest chair. His relaxed but piercing gaze met my eyes and looked at me from over the back of the chair. With a light smile and a dreamy English-accented voice, he said, "Hello." In response, I smiled back at him, stammered my own greeting, and swiftly retreated back to my dad's side. The actor was Jonathan Harris, but I only knew him as the creepy, crafty Dr. Smith from the television series *Lost in Space* (1965-1968). I wanted nothing to do with him. It's funny how even when you see perfectly kind actors in day-to-day life, their character is still smeared all over your interaction.

Yet, the Bewitched fun continued outside of the studios and on weekends. The chauffeur, Joe, would often drive the Ackermans, along with Bill Asher and Elizabeth Montgomery and their children, to Los Angeles Rams football games at the Memorial Coliseum. We'd all lounge together in the back of the stretch limo, laughing and having just the most absolute fun. Sometimes others would join us as well; one occasion being when Liz's brother, Robert Montgomery, Jr., traveled with us. As I recall, unlike others in the limousine, Mr. Montgomery was a more serious, brooding, individual. A moment I'll never forget in the back of Joe Fagan's limousine was when I actually saw Liz, just nonchalantly, wiggle her nose.

I think more fondly of that memory when I remember that once, on our way out of a Rams game, many people came up to her and asked her to wiggle her nose. She responded firmly but friendly, "Sorry, I don't do that, just watch the show!" Saying this after I'd seen her just moments earlier do that very action in the limo made me feel like I had that special connection to her. She was "Aunt Liz," and she didn't wiggle her nose for just anybody. After the game, while we ate and picked from endless choices of souvenirs, which was always my favorite part, us kids decided to do what little ones do so well—pester.

"Aunt Liz, can you wiggle your nose?" She just looked back seriously, saying, "ask me in the car." Once inside, as Joe drove us out of the stadium's parking lot, she told us sternly, but with a little more warmth, "I am going to do this once for you only. Do not ask me to do it again, because I will not, okay?" We boys, enraptured at what we understood was to be a rare spectacle, nodded our heads in agreement. Then, it happened. She wiggled her nose. I can confirm—it was not a camera trick. It just relied on a healthy, adept upper lip.

My mom and Liz were very close. Sometimes they'd stay behind as we went to the games, preparing dinner, laughing, and occasionally teaching one another to dance. In the process of learning a step, Liz twisted her ankle. I don't think her injury required any more attention than ice, but that was how we found them when Joe Fagan drove us home that day.

Joe seemed to be present for many of the strange experiences and odd interludes in our lives, including one that preceded the unknown at the time ending of *Bewitched*. Joe was driving mom and Liz to a pilot taping that my dad was executive producing, and Bill was directing. As the limousine drove down Sunset Boulevard, Liz suddenly stopped the flow of their conversation and yelled, "Joe, pull over now, please!" Mom was surprised and worried, and this was one of those moments where time sort of stops because you don't know what's wrong. Had she said something to upset Liz? Was she uncomfortable? Was this an emergency? It turned out to be none of those. Though Liz had been acting a little odd lately, my mom attributed that to stress. *Bewitched* was coming to a close because even though the network was putting forth many incentives to keep it going, by the seventh season, the plots became more ridiculous.

Maybe Mom was right and maybe it was stress, but I had to believe it had something to do with what I witnessed while on the

Bewitched set one day. (Don't worry, this story will come later). Whatever the reason, Liz told her to remain in the car as she hopped out and went into a jewelry store. She soon came back with a purchase, and as she settled back in the car and Joe took off towards the studio, Liz pulled out the bag. "Gifts for us," she said. They were two gold necklaces that Liz must have seen on a previous visit. And perhaps alongside having to keep a deep secret and knowing the type of woman that mom was, she had finally found the perfect person with whom to share this particular gift. The necklaces were identical with the exception of the engraving on each one. Liz clutched one to her chest and said, "This one is for me." Hers spelled out 'Naughty', while the one that she bestowed upon my mother said 'Nice'. "Because this is so you," Liz said. It wouldn't be until the messy conclusion of *Bewitched* that she would fully understand Liz's interesting gift and comment that she made.

As a boy, though, I reminisce on the time when Liz was family. She and her husband, Bill Asher, accepted the honor to stand as godparents for my baby brother, Chris. Six years older than him, I remember the private ceremony in the interior section outside a chapel at All Saints Episcopal Church, in Beverly Hills. The Episcopal priest who did the baptism honors, at some point asked Liz if she was going to wiggle her nose. Of course, she didn't, for him. Times were good, for sure, but they were about to change.

The Doomed Bewitched Set Signal

This day was a busy one for my dad, but I tagged along. He knew he could drop me off on the soundstage and all would be well. Things seemed the same as they did every visit. What made this visit extra special, though, is that I was left in the care of Aunt Liz and Dick Sargent.

In the first shot of the day, the principal actors are called in to be ready when the production crew is. There was still much to be done by the latter, so Liz and Dick Sargent sat doing what they did every morning; read the newspaper. It was always *The Los Angeles Times,* and they played the "Jumble" puzzle that was found within.

They invited me to sit with them in my dad's chair, his name emblazoned on the back. There I sat between these two icons of Classic Television as they each perused their puzzle. Jumble works like this… there are a few lines with jumbled letters. Out of each of those, you rearrange the letters to make a word. When finished, there is a final puzzle that includes a riddle. The letters to solve that final puzzle are the letters that are circled within the other answers that you've completed. Dick would ask me first to look at one of the early puzzle lines and see if I could figure it out. I was never able to, and to this day, it's just not my kind of puzzle. But he almost always could. When he wasn't able to, it seemed that Liz would solve it. They really were, on the set, like a husband and wife. They were two people very comfortable with one another, engaging in a "normal morning newspaper in the kitchen" kind of way. Eventually, they were called to set. Usually there are stand-ins used while the final lighting is adjusted, but for some reason that day, the two cast members were called in. Just before being called in, Dick was beside himself. He was so frustrated he couldn't get the final Jumble riddle answered. Liz said, "Let me see it," and try as she might, she wasn't able to solve it either. What happened next, I will never forget.

Before the director announced action, Liz said "Wait one minute, I just have to check something in my script!" She jogged across to where I was sitting and as she picked up her script out of the side pocket of the chair and flicked to a page, she whispered to me the riddle answer. "Don't tell Dick I told you," she stated as she turned and walked over to film the scene. I sadly have since forgotten the answer to that days' puzzle, but I felt infinitely special in that moment, having Liz share a secret. So, I did my part. Well, sort of. During break, Dick came back to his paper, which was on the seat next to me. I spoke up, "Hey, I think I figured out the answer!" He looked at each letter, the riddle, and finally said "You're right!" and without missing a beat, followed that with, "Liz told you, didn't she?" I think my smile gave me away; I could not keep a straight face back then. Liz play-scolded me a few minutes later, "You told him!" and I pleaded, "I tried not to!" That day started like this. It was fun and playful. However, this became a memorable day for an entirely different reason.

At the culmination of their next shot, Liz's character, Samantha, was supposed to faint in a restaurant where the scene took place, having been fed something that witches cannot eat. I sat in my director's chair and watched as actor Benson Fong portrayed the proprietor of the Chinese restaurant, who served Samantha a special drink to which she had a reaction. She would faint by spiraling down, with half of herself resting against Darrin's knees for a beat, and then safely collapsing the rest of the way to the floor. Liz was following this action from episode director, Richard Michaels.

After a few different shots, you could notice that her spiral downward ended with her bottom, albeit clothed in jeans, jutting out toward the camera and the director in a bit of a suggestive way. Michaels then said, quite loudly, "Oh, honey, I could watch you do that all day." The set became pin-drop quiet. As she got up and dusted herself off, she said something to Michaels that I couldn't hear, but I remember seeing that playful pixie smile on her face that was so Aunt Liz. Hearing him talk to her that way made me feel extremely uncomfortable. I mean, this was Uncle Bill's wife. We were on his and my dad's show set. I knew in a minute my mother would never put up with comments like that, but Liz did.

I was 11 years old at this time. It felt like a time where I began to leave childhood and understand how the world, especially the Hollywood world, worked. Our trusting that everything is as simple as we think begins to spiral, and at the same time, life begins providing clues to things we wouldn't have been able to previously identify or comprehend. There was something deeper between Michaels and Aunt Liz. It was there on set. I was sure of it.

I left my chair and walked away to other areas on the stage. I passed guest actor Bernie Kopell, who later played the Doctor on

The Love Boat, working on some business with the props that were handed to him for his scene. Still unable to shake what everyone else apparently took as a normal set interaction, I began wondering if my dad, or Uncle Bill, ever had these moments. Were they ever present to hear a comment like that? Did they ever come screen the daily film that was developed, and see and hear what I did? At the time I knew deep down something wasn't right, and I wouldn't be able to know for sure until a few days later at home.

Chapter 4

The Beginning of the End

That was my last time on the set of *Bewitched*, because the show's run concluded soon after. I learned about the end the way I began to learn a lot of things in my youth, by quietly listening. I was, back then, a tall and skinny boy who was shy and had the quietest manner. So much so that my mother nicknamed me "the shadow" because she would practically jump out of her skin when I, as she put it, "ghostly appeared" suddenly behind her.

One weekday morning, my dad wasn't dressed for the studio; that was different. He was in his robe and pajamas and slippers. He was standing away from the table at my mother's little work desk in the kitchen, talking on the telephone while my mom cooked them breakfast. I was just out of sight and used my shadow-like demeanor to become a fly on the wall. Dad hung up the phone with a, "Well, that is that" and sat down at the table. "The show is ending." My mother asked him why, as she delivered their breakfasts and joined him. "Bill and Liz are getting a divorce. That was her on the phone." Shocked, my mother again asked why, and my father told her even sadder news.

"Liz is in a love affair with one of our directors. ABC phoned her and the network wants her to continue to do the series, despite her impending divorce. Liz is willing but has one request; she wants Bill Asher out and this director in to become another producer on the show. I told her I can't do that to Bill. He is my partner and has been for many years. In light of my response, she informed me that *Bewitched* is over." I was crushed. That show wasn't just one that brought me such personal joy but was one with Uncle Bill and Aunt Liz. Who now weren't an "and" anymore.

A few days later, Uncle Bill came over with the kids, Bill (whom I knew as Willie back then), Robert, and Rebecca. I mistakenly, and now I see as foolishly, let the cat out of the bag when we kids were left alone, and I still wonder to this day if this was why Liz forbade them to ever come over to our home again. We were all outside by the tremendous free-standing treehouse in our backyard. There were different ways and locations on the structure to climb up and in. It had a slide along the side, and swings underneath the house. That afternoon we were swinging and playing all about the structure, buzzing like bees around a hive. Willie and I shared a ladder on the side of the treehouse where we took turns leaping off onto the grass below. As we were waiting to take our next giant jump, I brilliantly revealed what I knew. The consequence of what happened after— the Asher children being forbidden to play at our house— haunted me for decades after. I never revealed to my parents what I did; until now that I have told my mother while writing this book.

I asked Willie, "Do you know why your parents are divorcing?" He replied, "Yes, they sat us down and told us that they love us very much, and still like each other, but they don't love each other any longer and aren't going to stay married." How I wish I could go back and tell myself to keep my mouth shut. I had always looked forward to the visits from the Ashers. I remember teasing Rebecca mercilessly. I remember the rite of passage in our pool- our competition of forcing everyone to tread water for as long as they could. I remember years later at her dad's 75th birthday party when Rebecca said, "Yes, you tried to drown me!" How grateful I was to be forgiven for the past and for how we remain in contact to this day. While I miss the possible memories that might have come from us knowing one another more over the years, I'm glad to have the ones that I do.

I regret that after Willie shared what he was told, I inserted my side of his parents' separation reasons, like the knowledgeable, mature boy I was. "Well, I heard that your mother was in love the assistant director, and that's why she's not in love with your dad any longer." While Willie just shrugged, it must have been hard for him. Divorce was so foreign then to kids our age, and most families we knew didn't have them. I can only assume that Willie told his mother what I said because they were no longer permitted to visit. Just a few months later, it was Christmas morning which was a big deal in the Ackerman household. It was a day of mountains of gifts for each child, my mother's cooking, and the Asher's visit. On this day, I was told it would just be Uncle Bill with the kids. I couldn't wait. At some point in the late morning, a car drove up, and only Bill came to the door. As my parents welcomed him inside, my mother asked the obvious question, "Where are Willie, Robert, and Rebecca? I thought they were coming." Seeming uncomfortable as he answered her, Uncle Bill replied, "Sorry, Liz doesn't want the kids coming over here anymore." When my mother asked why, he just shrugged his shoulders, and looking back I assume this was the signal that they might talk about it later, but not in front of us.

For the rest of the day, I suspected that I might have been the reason. Perhaps Willie innocently revealed our conversation. Perhaps he was curious and wanted to know more. Perhaps it was also Liz's way of exacting some revenge on my dad for not continuing her and the show without Bill. Maybe Bill knew that and was protecting me, or maybe he had no idea. The Ackerman-Asher crew took its first hit then, not just with the divorce, but with the families' split up.

Though I held a small secret resentment against Bill (that I will discuss momentarily) for many years, I admired him that Christmas morning. He came with as much joy as he could, making it a memorable holiday for our family. His Christmas gift to me that morning is still something I cherish today. I can remember the very poor wrapping on the book-sized box he handed me. I chuckle remembering how the seams didn't meet, nor fully cover the gift, and tape was sloppily applied. It was a boxed set of the Sherlock Holmes paperback books. I would grow to become a mystery fiend and enthralled with everything the genre produced. This is something I credit not only to my being raised by reading-hungry parents, but to Uncle Bill, who gifted me with my first set of mysteries. I tend to find the good, even in situations that are less than perfect. Things were changing with *Bewitched* going off the air, but the next show my dad produced became a learning lab for me.

Harry Ackerman After Bewitched

At this point, I've taken you through (mostly) good times. You can see why I'm proud of both of my parents. It was always easier to see exactly what my mother did because she was on the screen and boldly in the credits. My dad, however, was a bit different. Sure, his name was also prominently displayed in the credits of his many television shows, but I was never quite sure what an Executive Producer did. I was led to believe it was a position for a fellow with money. In my dad's case, it was the studio's funds, not his own. His role appeared to be the best job ever. He walked around and greeted people and listened to others. But his life was so much more than that. It was fulfilling and challenging and most of it felt hidden.

In the early 1970s, Harry Ackerman was executive producing *The Paul Lynde Show* (1972-1973). *The Paul Lynde Show* was developed to, at the very least, fulfill the Bewitched contract, which was cut short from filming its final season by the sudden conclusion of the series caused by Liz Montgomery and Bill Asher's divorce. While the hope, with any show, was that it would continue for many seasons, sadly, this program only lasted the one season. Paul Lynde was the beloved comedian who guest starred on many shows, including *Bewitched* as Uncle Arthur, and made people laugh on the beloved, and my favorite, game show, *The Hollywood Squares*. After *Bewitched*, my dad and Bill Asher moved their creative project over to Paramount Studios. At this time, he was executive producing two shows; Paul Lynde's, which was filmed before a live audience, and a non-audience show called *Temperatures Rising/The New Temperatures Rising Show* (1972-1974). The latter was a comedy based in a hospital and starred Cleavon Little from *Blazing Saddles* (1974), and James Whitmore.

The Paul Lynde Show had a five-day schedule. This began with a read through and set building on Monday and concluded with the live audience taping on Friday. I spent the better part of a week watching the show unfold from the same empty area of the audience stands. Though my brother Brian was normally around on Mondays, I was solo Tuesday through Friday. I loved watching episodes as they developed and unfolded day after day. One of my favorite lines I heard on that set is one that I still use today. It's permanently ingrained in my brain, and I sometimes respond with it, not even thinking:

Howie (Paul Lynde's son-in-law): Long time no see, dad!

Paul: Not long enough!

Lynde's teen daughter was played by actress Pamelyn Ferdin, who was also starring on *Lassie* at the time. I had an enormous crush on her. That episode had Paul's older daughter and her hippie husband moving into a commune run by Ann Meara and Jerry Stiller (yes, Ben Stiller's parents); stars in their own right. My dad excitedly told me what a great comedy team Stiller and Meara were, and how lucky he was to have them on that episode.

Playing another young girl in the same commune was an actress I watched and pined over when she appeared on the television series *The Courtship of Eddie's Father* (1969-1972). Her name was Jodie Foster. From day one, my older brother and Jodie became close friends, and they would sit coloring pictures together all day. When I'd go to the studio, he'd always tell me to say hi to Jodie for him, but I just never could. While my brother was Mr. Bold, I was Mr. Hide Away and Make No Sounds. So, as I sat in the safety of my front row seat overlooking the cast and crew, I would sometimes sneak a look at Jodie and her mother who were sitting four rows behind me. At one point, I remember hearing Jodie cry, and I wondered if she was doing so because I would always avoid her and never say a word. Spoiler alert: it wasn't.

Still, hour after hour, and day after day, I watched Uncle Bill direct, do more formal positioning and stage movements, and later bring the cameras in for their blocking directions and more. It was eye-opening, watching the meticulousness and never-ending directorial responsibilities. Even though I most wanted to be an actor, I knew that I just wanted to work on television sets. Like every Harry Ackerman show, the crew appeared unified, happy, and worked together respectfully. Still, as with any film set, there were moments of tension.

Oh, Uncle Bill. How you have taught me so many lessons. The kind, sweet, smiling, friendly man could change instantly during a run-through. One day, there was a scene with the Lynde family seated around a breakfast table. Young Pamelyn missed her line, looking lost in a daydreaming gaze. It was only the second day of rehearsals, but Bill Asher exhibited the harshest, and what I believe to be uncalled for, retort I'd ever heard. "Come on, Pamelyn, wake up! Stop trying to think about what's going to happen to Lassie before next week and say your line!" Not only was it an overreaction in that moment, but Pamelyn was just a kid. Just like me. She teared up, but held her own through the rehearsal, and then broke down while sitting in her mother's lap after the scene ended. I remember her mom leaning down and whispering something encouraging into her ear. (Recently Pamelyn confessed to me that what her mom whispered then was, "now you know why he's getting divorced.")

As a kid, I saw Uncle Bill differently moving forward from that day. He was an adult I thought I knew, but whom I couldn't respect the same. This is what began my resentment, and as time passed, it just grew. In an unfortunate moment at a significant celebratory event years later, I would reveal my true feelings to him, something that I do regret today. Through adult eyes, I realize there was so much going on in his life at this point. He was angry and confused and hurt. He was struggling with divorce and single parenting. We were all growing apart. Unbeknownst at this moment, the Ackerman-Asher partnership was coming to an end. The conclusion of my dad's successful run came to a head after working on a couple of projects, one of those to fulfill the commitment to replace what was to be the final season of *Bewitched* with something else.

Though I hold many memories about that week on the set, one that stands out was not a pleasure, meeting, meeting Paul Lynde. On my first day, sometime after the morning run through where Bill blew up at a young actress, my dad arrived back onto the stage and walked me around to meet cast members and crew. Then he escorted me through dark areas of a soundstage, carefully stepping around equipment and over cables, to meet the famous Mr. Lynde. Lynde was different. It was true that he wasn't the biggest fan of children. With my father's reassuring arm on my back, he guided me towards where Lynde was sitting, reading his daily newspaper. "Excuse me, Paul," my dad said as a way of introduction. "I would like to introduce you to my son, Peter." Lynde's paper wilted just enough at the top so that he could get a good look at me. The sour lip downturn that worked so well in his comedy was there as he gave me a glance. I held out my hand and he merely looked at me, and then spoke with a dour, most insincere, perfunctory, and sneering, "Hello." Afterwards, he just sank back down into his chair. The signal that this was to be the conclusion of his greeting was the flick of his newspaper, as he opened it back up, with a sound as sharp as a car door slam. In a swift motion to make the awkwardness dissipate, my father guided me past Lynde and over to the many other actors who could cushion what was a less-than-pleasant encounter. I've had the joy of meeting some characters in my visits to television commercial productions, music video sets, and television days, but Lynde was definitely the first person I met where I saw that a person's public persona could be much different than the televised one. The studio where that show was filmed, became my newest show business playground.

Paramount Sets

While I grew up behind the camera, I found that most of my back lot adventures as a pre-teen and teenager happened at the magnificent Paramount Studios where I had many opportunities to visit, and have lasting memories, due to the times when each of my parents worked there. The amount of access I had on sets is still amazing to this day. In the late '80s and '90s, I saw studios become even more security conscious, where it was rare that you could just walk onto any stage or set, but that was my life at Paramount Studios!

Beginning with the *Paul Lynde Show* my dad spent some time at Paramount Studios, where he was kept on as an advisor, and because of that I still had plenty of time with my elementary school friends, playing on the lot, constantly trying not to get caught by the studio guards who would escort us back to dad's office. There was one guard in particular whose side constantly had me as its biggest thorn. He would always catch me playing on the studio's Western Street or hiding from him behind a pillar of a false front building. On these adventures, I became the grand tour guide, leading school friends through the lot. Two ever-important stops on my personal Paramount tour included the Western Street Saloon and the Property Department's gun rental shop.

The Saloon set on Western Street had typical swinging doors that were fun to walk through, though the real treasure lay inside. There was an empty bar in the cavernous chamber of the saloon, accompanied by dirt, dust, and darkness. Buried just a bit deeper was my grand surprise for any first-time guest who loved the television series. Kept inside was the giant telephone used in every 1960s series where people "shrunk" as part of the plot. Whether it was *I Dream of Jeannie* (1965-1970), *Bewitched*, or *Land of the Giants* (1968-1970), they all used this enormous telephone at one time or another. The phone, which was larger than a household couch, had a rotary dial on front, and we discovered we could lift the receiver off the cradle, though it was quite heavy and usually crashed to the ground. I ventured here every time I set foot on this particular lot; inside the Saloon façade, where the unused giant phone prop sat seemingly forgotten. It felt like my secret treasure, tucked inside my studio lot hiding place.

Additionally, there was what was known as Paramount Studio's Gun Shop. It was run by the Paramount Property Department but was in itself quite a museum. They were okay if you looked around as long as you touched nothing. A clearly posted sign stared at me each time I entered, "keep your hands in your pockets," which I always took seriously. The only item I was allowed to touch was a pistol made out of Styrofoam. It was a sample of what the shop could provide if a filmmaker wanted a realistic looking gun that an actor could use to hit another over the head with, while not causing any actual harm. Full disclosure—it worked. Many friends and I tested this sample, over and over again. While the property department was less than thrilled, I still can remember as I, with perhaps old friends Michael Olerick, Phillip Maple, or Paul Brown, did our Three Stooges imitation in that realm of wonder.

There were so many Paramount show soundstages that I visited over time. I remember watching *Happy Days* filmed before it was done so before a live studio audience. When dad had an advisory role on *The Partridge Family* (1970-1974), I was lucky enough to meet Shirley Jones. We chatted while she held a stack of dishes in her hands, prepared to film her reaction shots—this being when a director films non-spoken emotional shots of the performer. The director would instruct, "pretend you see Danny getting mud on his new trousers," and Shirley would cast a look of anger. The director would then say, "now you see David/Keith coming home with a lost puppy," and Shirley reacted appropriately, and so on and so on. She was a very sweet lady, and I adored her in my favorite film musical *The Music Man* (1962). One day on set with my school friend Phillip, we watched the scene from the shadows, and then while on break, David Cassidy invited us to sit with him. He could not have been any nicer. Cassidy strummed on his guitar and played us notes. "It's a song I am writing," he told us. I think back now and find it bizarre how normal I thought that was. My typical day included walking onto a soundstage, exchanging pleasantries with Shirley Jones, casually conversing with Ron Howard, or having a new song composed before me by David Cassidy. I know—what a very rough life.

While Paramount sets were fun and full of memories, there were times I wish we could forget. Eventually, Dad's contract at Paramount was up, and it wasn't renewed. In a very short time, I watched a man who was on top of the world, a man who worked for and with everyone who was beloved still in the industry—Sally Field, Liz Montgomery, Lucille Ball, and more—be unable to get a job. His family-oriented type of shows began to lose favor with studio executives and audiences. Though wonderful programs in their own right, my dad never quite understood the draw to increasingly violent police procedurals, or adult-leaning comedies, like *All in the Family*.

Whether he was aware of it or not, Dad made the unforgivable Hollywood sin of not reinventing himself. Instead, he stayed true to his stance on entertainment and the beliefs that had led him from radio to network head of West Coast Production, and eventually to Executive Producer. Luckily for him, his stance did favor him once again during his lifetime. He would be very proud to see his many contributions being appreciated today by the many viewers, such as yourselves, of the Classic Television networks. It was also with my dad where I said goodbye to a friend, not realizing at the time that it would be forever.

Fittingly, the last time I saw Elizabeth Montgomery was on a soundstage at a studio, Paramount. My dad was producing a couple of series on the lot and was also acting as an advisor to other shows in production. As we headed from one soundstage to another, he told me that he ran into Aunt Liz, who was also filming on the lot, and after learning of my upcoming visit, she asked my dad to bring me by to see her.

Perhaps because of an age restriction, I wasn't allowed onto the Lizzie Borden set. So, Aunt Liz came outside to see me. While she and I spoke, my dad stepped away to give us some visiting space. Speaking with her made it seem like everything was right in the world. She treated me as a confidant. She had that way of making me feel that we had a special bond, though I can imagine that was her way with everyone. She said, "Yesterday they closed this set because I had to film a nude scene!" She did a perfect pantomime; lifting one leg and using each one of her arms to cover sensitive areas on her torso.

Every so often she'd turn serious, speaking to me as an adult although I was just a boy in his pre-teens. We "talked shop" as she said. "Your father tells me that you are taking tap dancing lessons." She put her hands on her hips, and with the slightest of smiles, enticed me to perform for her. "Let's see what you've got!" she said. I began doing a beginner's move called a "shuffle step," which she recognized as such. Once my brief performance concluded, she was called back to set, and my dad and I left the stage to head to his next stop. She said goodbye, kissed my cheek, and though she would live for a long while longer, I never saw her in person again, or on film for that matter. I loved Aunt Liz, and know she is a great actress, but the idea of watching a post-Bewitched performance will remind me of the personal pain I experienced when she suddenly, and non-magically disappeared from my life. Still, at the time, we saw one another, it represented another fun adventure from my time at Paramount.

I spent time at that studio with my mother in a different way. She was always wonderful as a confidant, quietly providing me with some information as we walked across a soundstage set to meet someone; "He is sometimes very short with people, so don't be surprised." On the set of *The Odd Couple,* I chatted with the very friendly Tony Randall, and received a gruff, yet friendly, "hello" from Jack Klugman. On the set of *Happy Days*, on a soundstage I visited frequently when my father had an office at Paramount Studios, and well before it was filmed before a live audience, my mother had a role late in the series run and she introduced me to Henry Winkler, which was unreal. Ron Howard was always very approachable, and he could make a wardrobe change faster than anyone I have ever seen. He had a small dressing room on the stage. These were built out of wood and could be rolled where needed. Inside was a small desk with a lamp, and a couch big and comfortable enough to lie back on, but that was it. One day the director said, "Okay Ronnie, change out of the suit and tie and put on your school outfit with the letterman's jacket." In he went, and I'm serious, only about one minute went by and next thing I knew, the door swayed open and out comes Ron Howard in a totally different wardrobe. I asked him, "How did you get into these clothes so quickly?" He responded, "Oh I don't know, I guess you just learn to do it fast enough when you do it all the time." What a professional.

As a professional herself, my mother also worked frequently on the Paramount lot. She appeared on *Star Trek: The Original Series* and *The Odd Couple* (1970-1975), where she was cast as Miriam, Felix Unger's girlfriend. It was on the latter show that my mother met a Beatle! John Lennon was on what fans refer to as his "Lost Weekend," a multi-year stint in Los Angeles where he partied and recorded with many artists such as Harry Nilsson; played dad to Julian and lover to Yoko Ono's New York secretary, May Pang; where he laid down most of the tracks for what would become his rock n' roll album. One day, Lennon, Pang, Julian, and a friend of his came to Paramount just to look behind the scenes. He was escorted to two of Garry Marshall's shows-- *Happy Days* (where there is a picture with some of the cast members and Lennon, who looks retro cool in his leather jacket and round sunglasses) and *The Odd Couple* stage, where they were holding a dress rehearsal.

Lennon and company sat in the front row for the rehearsal. My mother remembers the buzz going around the crew. Eventually, a crew member asked her, "do you see who is here?" It was then she looked up and saw one of the most famous men at the time (and let's be honest, of all time) directly across from her. An endearing quality I find about my mother is that no matter what her age, she has always had that young fangirl quality inside her. Long ago at MGM, she asked for and received a signed photo from Peter Lawford, whom she had a major crush on (and whom I am partly named for). She used to carry an autograph book around to get celebrity signatures, and even now she is still an autograph seeker. One time while dining with Jane Wyatt at The Beverly Wilshire Hotel, Nancy Reagan and William F. Buckley were one table over. Jane and my mother spent considerable time debating whether they should ask for autographs, and in the end, decided against it.

Back to *The Odd Couple* set, my mother decided at this moment to go for it completely. She had constantly listened to The Beatles' *Revolver* album while pregnant with my brother James, and she ripped off a page from the back of her script and, with her own pencil with which she took staging notes and made dialogue changes, walked right over to them and said, "Excuse me, Mr. Lennon, can I have your autograph for my boys?" He was cordial and gladly agreed to sign and asked her for our names. Gifted to us later, we owned an in-person obtained pencil signature that read, "To Brian, Peter, James, and Chris…Love, John Lennon." His girlfriend at the time, May Pang, later told me more about that day in an email correspondence she and I had. Pang had recognized my mother right away and knew her from *Father Knows Best*. Alas, he had not. "Who is she?" Lennon had asked her. "Don't you know?" replied Pang, "That's Elinor Donahue!"

After we moved, my mother was cast in another pilot that went to series called *Mulligan's Stew* which was also filmed at Paramount. Unfortunately, this was helmed by Network President Freddie Silverman, who at the time seemed to throw every idea against the wall (or copy it) to see what would stick. Silverman even lobbied for a show about an orangutan as a business executive and *Supertrain* (1979), which was the channel version of ABC's *The Love Boat*. My mother's show, *Mulligan's Stew,* was NBC's version of rival network ABC's *Eight is Enough* (1977-1981).

In *Mulligan's Stew*, my mother played wife to the fine actor Lawrence Pressman as parents of a huge family. The basic plot was about a set of working parents trying to make ends meet while supporting a large extended family and tackling all their responsibilities. Suzanne Crough, who played the youngest daughter in *The Partridge Family,* returned to series television as one of the children, many of whom had ginger hair. When Johnny Whitaker (from *Family Affair* (1966-1971)) was replaced as the oldest child because he was believed to be too old for the part, a high school friend of mine, Johnny Doran, was cast in the role. While he did have a slight resemblance to my mom, she still thought I could have been cast. I guess we'll never know…

My mother allowed me to tag along to a photography studio where the cast was gathering to take publicity photos for the series. This session took place before any filming had begun, so it also served as a time for the cast to become reacquainted and for the returning members to meet new ones. Mom was whisked away into wardrobe, hair, and makeup as soon as we entered into the studio, and so I just hung around. Lawrence Pressman, a magnificent actor, walked over to me with a welcoming expression and immediately shook my hand, saying, "You must be my son!" I laughed and explained that while I sadly was not, I was actually Elinor's *real* son. Soon thereafter, Johnny Doran strutted onto set and the proper introductions were made. Where else but in Hollywood can a high school friend of yours play your own mother's fictional son? This connection also guaranteed more studio adventures at Paramount, where *Mulligan's Stew* was to be filmed.

Like the week I spent on the set of *The Paul Lynde Show*, my visits to the *Mulligan's Stew* set were fun and informative. I remember hanging out with Johnny when the set decorators were preparing his bedroom set. He had asked "Hey, I saw this great Fleetwood Mac Poster that would fit the back of the door, can you get it for my set?" "Sure!" the decorator replied, and I'm pretty sure they did.

Probably the best part of having a gregarious friend like Johnny was the access he could get me based on relationships he so easily forged with others. Although I was the one to introduce him to the gun shop over in the property area, he was way more comfortable conversing with actresses and talent. It was through hanging around and watching him that eased my anxiety over talking to women my age. Still, I was just as happy when it was him and me, with our conversations and adventures. He once asked me how I felt about *Star Trek*, to which of course I replied, "Love it!" I mean, who didn't like the show? I felt like I had an even deeper appreciation, with my mom having appeared on an episode, so the show was that much cooler to me.

"They are making a new movie and just started building the set, come on!" he said, leading me to a stage that wasn't far from *Mulligan's Stew*. When we walked on, there was a crew frantically working on a large set piece that looked somewhat familiar. "Hi, Johnny," one of the carpenter/technicians said. Johnny introduced me and the man showed us what he was working on.

"See here, I am putting in little lights all along these displays." And with those in place, he lit them up, all of them starting to blink and twinkle at different speeds. That's when I realized that we were standing on the bridge of the Starship Enterprise! It was so close to being finished, and I could see the various crew stations beginning to come together, the seating area for the captain, and more. Next to being on the *Batman* set, this was a huge thrill for me, and probably one of the reasons I'm one of the few who is partial to *Star Trek: The Motion Picture*. When I see the movie, I can look at the bridge and think to myself, "I was there!" Along with all these good memories, come the remembrance of my dad's vocational challenges.

Setbacks

In a creative vocation, such as television, there will always be setbacks. In what I think was the first blow to his career in an otherwise stellar period was the cancelation of *The Ugliest Girl in Town* (1968-1969). At the time, ABC was so happy with the output supervised by my father as they began to prepare their fall schedule. They didn't feel the need to put anything more than the words, "A Harry Ackerman Show" in a particular slot, knowing that he would deliver.

Of all of the pilots that never went to series, the one I was heartbroken over was called *Inside O.U.T.* (1971). The show was from Dad's specialty – a half hour comedy pilot that featured various actors including my favorite "Tarzan," Mike Henry. Also in the cast was the then-yet-unknown actress in her pre-*Charlie's Angels* (1976-1981) days, Farrah Fawcett. They portrayed members of a Mission Impossible-type team of secret agents who hid in plain sight with regular jobs in the community. Henry, as a furniture mover, would suddenly be called into his secret agent role, immediately abandoning his mover partner who was left holding one end of a sofa. Fawcett was a museum docent who said, "Follow me this way," to those on a tour with her, and when she received the call to go into the agency, she would begin running, causing her tour group to confusedly follow. It was full of gags and chuckle moments, and while I was personally disappointed the show wasn't picked up as a series, little did I know it was more so because the classic days of quirky television comedies were being replaced by new kinds of entertainment.

Another cast-aside pilot was an attempted spin-off from the film *Cat Ballou* (1965). It was the public's reception of the program that night that would determine the fate of the pilot. Honestly, all I remember about the event was that the souvenir cowboy hat I wore that promoted the program served very useful as a school friend of mine who attended the premiere with me got sick and needed something to get sick into. That is probably the most-telling outcome I could paint you of how that premiere went.

However, despite that thoroughly gross encounter, there is another show I feel was worse. In my humble opinion, *The Ugliest Girl in Town* was asking to be cancelled. It predated the sitcom *Bosom Buddies* (1980-1982) and the film *Tootsie* (1982) and was about a fellow who could only get hired by pretending to be a woman. On top of that premise, it was filmed in England with British actors, and I'm still unclear as to why. All I do know is that Dad was gone for long stretches at a time while this show was in production. Though a fair amount of his energy went into this show, I never visited sets or knew the actors. Of all his shows, this is one produced during my lifetime to which I felt zero connection.

These multiple pilot failures, combined with the cancellation of *The Flying Nun* and the cessation of *Bewitched* began the major downward spiral of my father's career. It just kept piling on as he and Bill Asher split after the conclusion of *The Paul Lynde Show* and when my father was released as the Executive Producer of *Temperatures Rising.*

I never had the opportunity to truly ask my father about this period in his life, but I always sensed the split with Bill Asher broke him deeper than he let on, despite his normally stoic and gentlemanly manner. Bill essentially stepped out of his director's chair and went on to helm *The New Temperatures Rising.* An unanswered question for me is if Bill knew of my dad's loyalty to him—specifically speaking to the opportunity he had to carry *Bewitched* forward without Bill—with the prompting and encouragement of Elizabeth Montgomery. The way I saw it, the loyalty was one-sided. Given the opportunity, Bill did move forward without his partner.

On one side, Bill Asher personified a contemporary who adapted with the tides of change. In the mid '70s, he continued to work and thrive, directing shows like *Alice* (1976-1985). He was still in our family picture, coming to our house for visits, laying bets on football games, and attending dinner parties. However, on the other side, because of the disloyalty that I perceived, I grew a resentment towards Bill, but if my father had any, he was able to put it aside.

It was through this period of setbacks where I learned just how tough show business was. I was born at the height of their careers, and just as soon as I became old enough to understand how fragile fame could be, things began to change for my dad, and thus for us, his family. In short, finances became tight, because as I realized, though shows made by or featuring one of my parents were still on television, that did not mean that there were large dollar amounts coming in.

There is certainly glamor in Hollywood, but I also know of the grit. Today's actors have it better, by far. Just look at "residuals," which is the money one receives for additional viewings of a program that they appeared on. Over time, they lessen to mere pennies. Episodic television viewers forget that though we see the same shows, like *Star Trek: The Original Series*, shown over and over, year after year, the actors who worked minimally and might now be out of work, are no longer receiving pay for their performances. This was all too clear on one of those *Mulligan's Stew* days when I walked around Paramount. A dilapidated old car drove through the lot's main gates one day, and while it passed me, I saw the driver was actor DeForest Kelley, who was probably arriving for a wardrobe fitting for his part of Dr. McCoy on *Star Trek: The Motion Picture*. I knew all too well that though the shows continued to air, the funds did not necessarily continue to flow. I'm glad that with autograph shows and more, cast members of Classic Television series have been able to generate additional earnings for their work. Having a show canceled is a hard thing. With my father not working, I know *Mulligan's Stew* was a godsend. And so did my mother. It was a series that gave her a chance to earn enough to support all of us, keep good health insurance, and served as a boost of some much-needed capital in the Ackerman coffers. Yes, there's money in Hollywood. But it's never guaranteed.

The stress felt by my parents in their vocational roles began to appear in the mid-1970s. For a while, my mother tried her hand at working on television commercials. It was not a great experience for her. One commercial was for cat food. She spent all day doing what is said to be the worst in show business – working with animals AND children. She was portraying mom to a couple of youngsters who were begging their finicky feline to eat. The culmination of the shot was when they put down the advertised product and the cat went right to it and began gobbling it up, with Mom exclaiming, "He's eating!" while hugging the kids, the strains of *Stars and Stripes Forever* playing. It was a cute spot, but difficult. One of the kids was a regular on a television series at the time and was known to have a bit of an attitude. His lack of an on-set professional behavior got to my mother, though she never let on.

Adding to that headache was the fact that she spent a great part of her day working with a cat and had to attempt every variation possible of her line, "He's eating!" Like I said, there's definite grit to Hollywood glamour. There were few days where there'd be a perfect storm of repetitive challenges, and that didn't bode well for me when she got home, as I was the same age as her not-so-professional child costar, and the stress of that day was still weighing heavy. I'd give her a "hello," and next thing I remember she'd be yelling at me to keep quiet. After any snap, she always apologized. She'd explain her day and get it off her chest, and I would always be there to end the night laughing with her over it all.

Dad's career chugged along. He was tied to a couple of projects in the '80s; he voraciously read scripts and worked on story ideas with Bob Dwan who had once been a writer for Groucho Marx. He worked on developing shows, yet the home life began to become a bit strained in those days. There were all too painful reminders around my dad feeling forgotten by the industry. Though there was no jealousy or competition evident between my parents, my mother was clearly doing rather well at the time, performing as a series regular on *The New Adventures of Beans Baxter* (1987) and *Get a Life* (1990-1992), while starring in plays around the country. When television is the medium that seems to have left you behind, watching it becomes a painful experience. And television is everywhere. Even before streaming was a concept, everyone was constantly glued to TV.

"This show is filmed/videotaped before a live studio audience." Some form of this statement accompanied almost every television program in the '70s. This phrase twisted like a knife in the gut of my father, who knew he was the reason a show was filmed this way but was forgotten or cruelly and purposely left out of the three-camera technique credit. I answered the phone one day when Desi Arnaz phoned for Harry Ackerman. While my brother went to find him, I stayed on the phone with Mr. Arnaz, who was wonderful at making conversation with a boy who he knew to be relatively shy.

I was always grateful for that. "So…Peter…do like the horse races?" I remember him asking me and I remember being so comfortable when talking to him. He had called to let Dad know in advance that he was going to solely claim the three-camera technique credit in a book he authored, which was about to be published. Arnaz and Dad went way back, including sharing a love of fishing in the deep waters off of Mexico. I know decisions like the one Arnaz made hurt Dad, but he was a kind man. Dad refused to let the bad parts of business tarnish the good ones with friends. I don't know how he did it.

As the years went by, however, I could see Dad becoming more sensitive to the feeling that he was forgotten or underappreciated. I remember one story my dad once told of his date with Marilyn Monroe. He was set up by a friend for a blind double date and all went well until they hit the dance floor. "Suddenly" Dad told me, "Out of nowhere, flashbulbs started going off and we couldn't see a thing. All we could do was return to our seats." To this day, I search for that possible lost Marilyn photo, perhaps one featuring an unknown dance partner, in the hopes of discovering a visual aid to this story. Here was a guy who, besides all of the work he did for television entertainment was not even remembered as having a date with Marilyn Monroe. Not that anybody would, especially with the lack of evidence available, but it contributed to his feeling of marginalization by an industry that once embraced him.

By the 1980s, even innocent speeches from actors made him feel forgotten. My first encounter with Sally Field is as warm a memory as my last is a victorious one. We were hosting a huge Hollywood party at our home. Dad was carrying me out to tuck me in bed, when he stopped to bring me over to a woman who I had seen on television. "Do you know who this is?" he asked as he introduced us. Very shyly I looked at her and said, "Yes, it's Sister Bertrille." She fawned a bit over me and that was that.

Being that young, I still saw people in life as they were on television. I was delighted over the years to learn from my dad about what went on behind the scenes. Dad recalled how during the early days of *Gidget* he nurtured a nervous young actress who was ready to quit on her first day of filming. Field was recently discovered and was about to go film scenes as the lead and her nerves had her wanting to run. So, she ran to my dad. He assured her, "You were chosen for this part because we know and saw that you have what it takes. You're not doing anything that you haven't already done." With that nurturing and kindness, she went on and began making a name for herself in the industry.

Field went from television to movies. She had much well-deserved attention for her work in various kinds of films, from *Norma Rae* (1979) and *Smokey and the Bandit* (1977), to *Places in the Heart* (1984). When she received the Academy Award for one of her films, I remember our whole family sat in the TV room and watched as events unfolded. It was Sally, on our television screen, approaching the dais, about to accept an Oscar. I carefully glanced over at my parents who were strangely quiet. Dad sat erect in his favorite chair, which creaked as he shifted his weight forward. His eyes were locked on the screen, intently watching and listening. On the couch next to me, my mother's hands were turning pale as she had every finger crossed that she could. My parents were waiting for recognition.

Sally Field walked up and began her speech, at one point saying something along the lines of, "and I would not be here if not for one man…. Burt Reynolds." I still feel a twinge in my stomach for my dad. He had been such a key supporter of her career, as he had been with so many others. I know she didn't mean any harm, and winning an award like that will fluster everything about you, but it just highlighted that feeling he had at the time, that slowly he was being cast away, forgotten, and how he hoped for recognition. Not for his ego, but to confirm what we all knew to be true; he made a difference in the television industry. Sally Field's speech came at a time when my out-of-work father was craving a notice of any proportion. Following that night, our television was switched off. It was then I truly understood how easy it was to be forgotten in this industry, even if you helped birth it.

Though public acknowledgement for his contributions eluded him for many years, the fact remains that Harry Ackerman was central to the development of so many shows and memorable classic characters. In her book, Sally Field writes about speaking with my dad on broadening her character to become more than a two-dimensional nun who flies to instead be someone whom the audience knows through a backstory. He worked with everyone around him to help develop this and to write episodes with deeper social associations, as my dad and his team were already implementing on *Bewitched.* Part of adding a backstory to the life of Field's character was the introduction of her fictional older sister, Jennifer, who was played by my mother!

At one of Field's live appearances at the Sixth and I Synagogue in Washington D.C. to promote her autobiography, there was a question-and-answer period where I was able to introduce myself to her. After I stepped up to the microphone, I let her know who my (at this time, late) father was and the audience went wild. That spontaneous emotional eruption was, for me, validation enough. Her audience was actually cheering for my father and celebrating his shows, two of which she was fortunate to be a part of. Though I don't believe she recalls as fondly of how my father's story intersects with hers, at least there is a great appreciation by her fans for *Gidget* and *The Flying Nun.* She had the last word as I left the microphone that evening. After chatting and reminding her of that party at my home, she said, "My, you've grown!" She proved in those moments why my dad was right in having her cast in the lead of those shows. She was kind. Regardless of that night at the Academy, right here was that moment of redemption my father always wanted. It was during this uncertain time around their careers that I began high school, where my own uncertainty in identifying what I was going to do with my life, took a confirming turn.

Chapter 5

Notre Dame High School – Where I Became Me

The pull of show business that I felt from when I was a child solidified during my high school years at Notre Dame High School in Sherman Oaks, California. This pedagogical place impacted me more than I ever thought possible. It was there at Notre Dame High School where I truly discovered who I was.

First, it was the location where I met my best friends, with whom I am still close today. At the time I attended, Notre Dame was a school for men only, and the first person I met was a kid named Brian, as we nervously held onto our trumpet cases on the way into our first school band rehearsal before the fall semester began. Another eventual friend, Paul, and I met while waiting for the bus. It was when he excitedly showed me his latest album purchase. The record was the latest, and second release, from a then-upcoming group known as Van Halen. Little did we know that was just the beginning of the Van Halen records produced, and concerts scheduled. Paul may have even gone with me one of the times I saw Van Halen. My mother guest starred on an episode of a popular television series called *One Day at a Time* (1975) that co-starred a young woman who dated and later married the guitarist and band member Eddie Van Halen. Through that connection, I was able to score some great show tickets. What makes this memory even more wonderful is that many years later, Eddie and Valerie's son, Wolfgang, would be a graduate of our same high school.

Finally, I was introduced to Paul and Brian's friend Danny who rounded out our tight friendship circle. Danny and I have a deep and special connection that I will always cherish. I became his godfather when he was baptized, and he is the godparent of my son, Harry. Additionally, around the same time, when in our thirties, Danny and I each felt ourselves tugged into the direction of new careers, with him settling in law enforcement and me in ministry. During our four years at Notre Dame, there were others I grew close with and then lost touch with through life, but these three men were, and still are, my very best friends.

When I began leaning deep into the desire to pursue performing arts, the campus library at Notre Dame High School became a central place of exploration for me. To be honest, I'm not sure that I accessed an academic work from the stacks, but there was still plenty there to interest me. I still remember the beloved glass case positioned near the entrance. This special bookcase had sliding glass panels that were kept locked by the librarian Miss Trippi. Encased within were larger pictorial volumes and coffee table books. For me, this is where the best volumes were kept, those works that were for show business and had movie-related content. Inside were volumes containing plenty of photos of the films of creators such as W.C. Fields and the Marx Brothers. One could only check out one of the glass-encased treasures at a time, and I believe it was for one night only, unless you checked it out for the weekend. Like-minded students would sometimes plan which volumes each would check out so that we might share and look through them together. I remember passing by friends in the halls as we switched classes and sizing up which volume we each scored for the weekend.

I perused every page. I soaked up every ounce of information; of the photos too, as if I was studying an ancient Egyptian artifact (which I believe is what my parents probably wished I was doing). Whether it was to see what W.C. Fields looked like later in life without his drinker's nose covered in make-up, or how Groucho Marx's look changed over the years with a fake mustache becoming real and a balding head suddenly donning a toupee. It was these photo-filled volumes that immersed me further into show-business history, and boy was I enraptured completely.

Then, there was *the* book, which was my favorite in the library, *Ventriloquism for Fun and Profit*. I wonder if the "variety arts" (puppetry, dance, comedy routines in teams or solo, singers, magicians, etc.) that were performed in vaudeville where my mother got her start were in my blood. I was drawn to them all–the history, the performers, the artistry–and it was a yearning I kept going after. In Notre Dame's well-stocked library, I was able to discover more about variety arts and this is what led me to ventriloquism (I know, I know. I was the coolest). What I loved about it then, and still enjoy today, is that it gives a voice and opportunity for shy and quiet kids (and adults) to feel comfortable speaking up. For those who need that push or outlet, it was an opportunity to grow confidence; to have fun and melt public anxiety away simultaneously. I watched ventriloquists at work and saw how the performer was able to jump from being rude to flirtatious, and get away with it, by having a puppet speak those words. Within a certain level of respect, the ventriloquist could say what they wanted, even taking the time afterwards to chastise the puppet for a set, which made it all the more fun.

Though I can't recall how many times I checked it out, I believe I was the only student in my four years to access the treasure known as *Ventriloquism for Fun and Profit* by ventriloquist and voice artist, Paul Winchell. Part biography, part how-to, with some added anecdotes about how-not-to, this autobiography provided me with rudimentary lessons on how to speak without moving my lips. Though I'm not perfect, I still practice ventriloquism today, and can very much hold my own through it. Rather than wondering aloud to myself while driving my car, or silently singing while I am on a morning jog, I will frequently use ventriloquism so that I'm not caught talking to myself. Isn't that what everyone does?

Pushing past industry how-to and history lessons, my fiction reading was often anchored in movies and television as well. I read a lot. I loved mysteries, spy thrillers, and show business biographies. However, my favorite fiction works were the movie-tie-in novelizations that were frequently published at that time. Again, because it wasn't easy to just pop-in your favorite movie for yet another viewing, my books held great importance to me. If you wanted to experience the movie *Jaws 2* (1978) after its theater run concluded, you could pick up and read the tie-in novel of the film. Added to this luxury was the reward.

This immersion into various areas of show business during high school helped me to understand and deepen my desire for it, and it was while I was a student at Notre Dame High School where I took some of my first opportunities to perform. On stage, whether it was at Notre Dame High School or our all-girls sister school Corvallis, I performed in various plays and musicals. I will be very honest here; I was not good. At first. But I became better over time. It was my parents who, when they came to see me in my second high school play, noticed the new me stepping out of the shadows. My mom often reminds me of the time she and my father went to see their sometimes sullen, always quiet-with-his-nose-in-a-book teenager in a school production of *The Sound of Music*. The bar for what they expected to experience was low, but they were there to support me. When I came out on stage as Rolf, the telegram messenger boy who sings about turning from 16 to 17 with the character Liesel, my parents were amazed that the person on the stage was that same sulky teenager who lived day in and day out with them. He had presence and could actually sing. They saw a side of me that, until then, I kept in reserve. It was beginning to be easier for my parents to see that I might have a chance as a performer, as life in high school helped me figure out who I was; helped me grow and become someone I was happy to be.

Besides performing, I did what it took to work on a high school production. At first, at my very own high school, I found it difficult to get cast. It was probably, in that period of time, that I began to consider working towards a goal, rather than awaiting a lucky shot. After seeing who got cast, people who were usually well regarded by the director, who was also the English teacher who had them in class. Through no fault of my own, I had the misfortune of not being assigned to *his* English course, so I took matters into my own hands. Instead waiting for the next show's casting session, I approached the faculty member, Mr. Cser (pronounced Caesar), an intimidating person for a high school sophomore. He had a booming voice and looked as wide as he was tall. But, I moved past my fear and asked him if there was something else that I might do behind the scenes of the current production. Surprised, as he thought I was coming to him to beg for a role he already assigned to another, he took me on as the stage manager, though with a healthy ego, I called myself "assistant director!" It was a good production, and the relationship helped Mr. Cser get to know me and my dedication to theater arts. In my senior year, I had the pleasure of performing in *Guys & Dolls*, where I played one of the two roles I always wanted to play: Sky Masterson.

When my stint as stage manager came to an end, Mr. Cser asked me to buy flowers for the talent that we would present before the final evening's performance. I went to my local florist and encountered Mr. Lynch, whose own headshot hung on the wall of his establishment. Ken Lynch was a former working actor who ran the flower shop in his retirement. Sympathetic to my situation, he worked with my budget and helped me to purchase one red rose for each member of the cast and crew. He stopped and asked me, "You have a leading lady, don't you?" I nodded yes, and he told me, "It's important to keep her special," and then handed me a white rose, with some decorative spray around it. His lesson that day remained a valuable one on how to treat talent, whether in a high school production or on a professional television set.

The other notable performative experience for me at Notre Dame happened in my senior year. Today, I proudly claim that like Johnny Carson and George W. Bush, I was yell leader. A yell leader is the male counterpart to the female cheerleader. These men need athletic and tumbling skills and work with their counterparts who stand on their shoulders and dismount in thrilling ways. Young women from the private and public schools around us would audition to become cheerleaders for our school. In my senior year, the head coach decided to offer opportunities to join this squad to people who had any kind of performance ability or desire, regardless of if it was through an athletic program. In previous years, yell leaders often seemed to be guys who were too injured to play football. But fortunately for me, the coach opened up this possibility, and it resulted in a very interesting group coming together. There were those of us from our senior class: me, a fellow who had been in the marching band for a year and now did stage plays, my very friendly and very tall friend Paul, a shorter bundle of energy named Gene, and Chris, a stellar academic. For a while, our male crew also included a couple of underclassmen, John and Matt, before an injury took out one and a rigorous study schedule the other.

Yell leading was a blast, and just like other performing traits I garnered around this time, offered me some early experiences that are oddly similar to what I do vocationally now. Yell and cheerleaders need to interpret the events happening on the field of play. They encourage the crowd to hang in there during slumps and offer themselves up as a conduit between the fans and the players and vice versa.

Finally, my senior year concluded as a storybook one for me. Co-starring with talented fellow students in my high school's production of *Guys and Dolls* and yell leading were just some of what I got to experience. One more story for you: I learned a lot about fundraising and how incredibly helpful it was to call on celebrities for assistance. I remember being on our school's committee to promote a dance-a-thon to raise money for the Muscular Dystrophy Association. Interested students from our school and the all-girls school near us signed up to dance for twelve hours beginning at 9 in the morning until that evening. Someone else took the role of getting a sound system and dance records. For me it was lining up celebrity guests to entice attendees to participate. This was probably the first time in my life where I used the connections that I was blessed with to make the event a successful one. With the help of my mother, who appeared as one of our celebrity guests, I was able to get Dick Sargent from my dad's show *Bewitched*, where Dick was the second actor to play the homemaker witch's husband, Darrin, and Rue McClanahan, who was later known for her role in the hit television show *The Golden Girls* (1985-1992), a sitcom about three old ladies who lived together At the time, Miss McClanahan had recently concluded her work as a series regular on *Maude* (1972-1978),a spin-off of All in the Family, about an older independent woman living in New York, with Rue playing the lead character's best friend. My mother knew Rue from their working together on stage.

By the time I graduated from Notre Dame, I had gone from a shiveringly shy, poor-playing trumpet player to becoming a quite popular performer. I remember the surprise I felt when one of the members of the football team came over to me at a school dance to introduce me to his girlfriend. This small action brought a new world of confidence to me that I did not have as a freshman. I learned about the differences between my public identity and personal one. I not only liked who I was, but also felt comfortable in my own skin, which is not an easy win for a teenager.

My stage work continued for a few years after I graduated, as my next educational stop was very theater heavy.

College Acting

Having fallen in love with stage acting in high school, I focused on that art when I attended college. With that in mind, I decided in the fall of 1980, at 18 years of age, to attend Los Angeles Valley Junior College (LAVC) which had a stellar theater program. I figured that after doing my undergrad work there for a couple of years I would either continue my schooling at a university or focus solely on acting. Little did I know at the time that it would take me 18 years from leaving the junior college before beginning at a university as a junior to obtain my degree.

Beginning in the fall of 1980, The Los Angeles Valley College Theater Arts Department became my home for the next three years. I took my theater training seriously. My favorite instructor there was a man named John Larson who also cast me in a few of his shows. My first course with Mr. Larson was in voice training. That's where I learned to emote. To this day, I can enter into a large auditorium, or in the case of my current vocation, a church, and be heard across the room without a microphone. This talent was achieved due to both his teaching and my dislike of being touched.

Early on in the class, to teach students how to relax their bodies and rely on their diaphragms to push out their voices, Mr. Larson had us lay on the ground on our backs. By this time, we had all memorized a Shakespeare sonnet and he had us, one by one, recite it from this odd position. Mr. Larson knelt down by each student as they spoke. If someone wasn't using their diaphragm to emote, he would use his two hands to firmly push down on the individual's stomach to show how it feels to use that part of the body. This taught us to use our air reserve, not just our vocal cords. The stomach muscles pushed out speech in a manner that amplified the voice. I was adamant that I was not going to let this relative stranger put his hands on my stomach, so I focused on the technique like my life depended upon it. Sure enough, I grasped the concept, emoted well, and he never laid a hand on me. He even used me as an example to the rest of the class of how it should be done.

I met many talented friends from those theater arts years, some of whom still act. One of whom actually "made it" and is now forever a part of popular culture, Larry Thomas, is a marvelous actor in any role. Fortune smiled upon him some years after leaving the department when he was cast for an episode of *Seinfeld* (1989-1998) as the "Soup Nazi." Others had some regular work after their training at LAVC, including actor Michael Milhoan who if you don't know by name, I guarantee you have seen in many television shows, films, or commercials since the early 1980s.

My immersion in theater went further than just acting in plays, which I did plenty of over my three years in the department. I acted on the huge main stage, using the learned skills of voice projection and relaxed and intimate presence that should accompany stage work. My favorite venue, however, was the theater in the round, a location where there was no hiding or turning away from the audience. The actor was in the middle of spectators, and I loved the sensation of the closeness to the viewers. It was there that I experienced my one great show moment save.

The play was called *Dr. Hero*, and it was a true ensemble piece with a cast of about ten playing various roles throughout the show. One scene took place at a cocktail party. In the center of the floor, six of us stood exchanging our lines, which were delivered in quick staccato with each actor's line following the other. One night, one of the actors forgot where he was in the script and accidentally spoke a line of his own from later in the scene. The next actor spoke his later line as well, while a third performer knew we were off-script and tried to salvage the skipped dialogue. That confusing combination broke the rhythm and suddenly no one knew what to do next, and the audience, still oblivious to the error in progress, simply watched us. I give credit to my growing up in the business that allowed me to stay relaxed in that moment where everyone began to slowly panic.

I identified where we went off the printed page and took us back. I spoke the line that was originally missed, I pointed to the person who had the line after him and said his line, and then pointed to the next person and said hers. I then put my palm on my chest, said my own scripted words, and finally I pointed to the actor who followed me. That was what we needed to get us back into the piece. After we exited the stage, they all gratefully thanked me for saving our scene. It felt good to be of service, a feeling that I still get to have in my current vocation. Working in a church, whether it's a Sunday service or a funeral, I arrive early and run through my expected movements and words for the service. I become comfortable in the space. I continually thank my parents, who always let me know through not only words but actions that show business was never about one person, but about all of us.

On my last show at LAVC, I received the greatest acting compliment I would ever get, and it was from my dad. It was during a comedic scene from a play whose title unfortunately escapes me. When performing a live comedic piece, there are many moving parts that can change how it's presented each night. There are the basics: know your lines, be familiar with movement, anticipate anything. However, the audience and their response play a big part. Laughter is something a performer can inadvertently cut short by moving past the moment too fast or lose by letting a wave of laughter last too long before moving to the next scene. Timing is everything, and it can't be taught. It's an intuition; my intuition, which helped me ride and guide the waves of laughter.

I was actively furthering my interests in following my parents' footsteps, and while it may have been reluctant before, their support was now, in the early 1980s while I was at college, becoming active. After a performance of that show, my dad took me aside and said to me "Peter, I have worked with some of the comedy greats. Lucy (Ball) and Jack Benny knew comedic timing, and so do you. You cannot teach it, you have to have it, and you do!" I will never forget that moment. It was one where I knew that my dad, who was very reluctant about my decision to go into performing, was proud of me. In fact, not too long before he died, when I told him I was looking to leave my Hollywood dream, the man who tried to talk me out of going into it in the first place encouraged me to remain in.

It was while at Valley College, though not because of it, that I received my first on cameral gig. My older half-brother's wife at the time, Francine Selkirk, who was producing a commercial for a smoke-less ash tray, cast me as an extra. Filmed at a palatial home that was once part of the silent comedian Harold Lloyd's vast estate, the spot starred beloved actor and comedian George Burns. Standing with other extras when Mr. Burns arrived, ever-present lit cigar in hand, he accepted our welcoming applause and then gazed up at the grand home and property before us. He then learned towards us and asked, "Did you know that when Harold Lloyd bought this property, it only cost him about five thousand dollars for the whole thing?" We were amazed at that tremendous number and told him so. The ever-serious man, having once been the stern side of a comedy duo that featured his wife Gracie as the funny one, Burns was really waiting for the right response, which finally came from another extra who replied to his information about the astronomically low purchase number with a "Really!?" Burns took a beat with a hearty puff of his stick, and as he blew out the smoke he smiled, and said "nah," and turned from us and walked away to his dressing room. We all had a treat at that moment. He gave us a healthy dose of his humor and left us laughing. That moment was a great opportunity for me to see an artist work effortlessly at his comedic craft.

Around that time, having received my two-year degree, it became time for my next step. The choices were before me, finish college, or be an actor. Guess which route I chose?

My Struggling Actor Period

By the time I left Valley College, I decided to devote myself full-time to becoming an actor. So, as one does, I began waiting tables. What became clear over the next few years was that while I loved the stage, the camera was not for me. Today, there are classes for that intricate performance art, but they were not so easy to find in the early 1980s.

To be honest, my auditions were over the top. Even when I was cast in a small part, the director often had to spend time attending to me, something a director does not want to do with an actor who only has one or two lines. Often the advice was to pull back on my emoting. I adjusted as I could, but it was always a challenge moving away from my stage training. Additionally, film acting had a lot of waiting around. I liked the stage where a role was not done once it was performed, but fresh each and every time it was delivered. I didn't have to wait an hour or more to get in front of the camera again.

Auditioning for roles was so frustrating that the experience became laughable. At the time, I was sent in to see a casting director for a small part in a show or film, usually as the best friend to the lead. Every audition I would see the same fellow actors, all who had similar features to me, also reading for the part. One of them, a man whose name I never knew, was often cast in these parts.

At other auditions, I remember this one guy, always looking for his next role, who used to appear in the casting office and move to the front of the line. Scott Baio, who had been on *Happy Days*, and later a spin-off of the first show, *Joanie Loves Chachi* (1982), would always walk in and then get taken immediately into the back room where the casting session was taking place. In quick order he would do his audition and leave. It was frustrating for us actors in the waiting area, for sure. I remember feeling that the part I usually read for, some version of a "funny college buddy," was right up my alley, both in talent and looks. It was challenging enough walking into a casting office and seeing a half dozen or more fellows that looked similar to one another. And then to have an established actor walk in the door and move to the front of the line was not a fun turn of events. Still, in show business, it takes a lot of resolve to get into and stick with it. I am certain I never was cast in one of these roles, but then neither was Scott! In the end, I never begrudged an actor using a professional relationship or fame, to get into a door. It is part of what makes the industry interesting!

In an attempt to advance my skills, I was sent by my agent to take a special auditioning class. During the third week of the course, the teacher saw something in me and decided to test her theory. She called me up front, thrust a few script pages in my hand, and told me which part to read. It was a script from a popular situation comedy, probably *Happy Days*, and I did the best I could with the words in front of me for the first time.

Then the instructor switched scripts and asked another actor to come up and read with me. This time she gave us copies of a play by Chekov and indicated to us the parts we were to read and told us to begin. When class was over, she took me aside and said "You have an interesting problem; something that is usually the other way around for actors. When you read comparatively trite television scripts, you come off like a fish out of water. When you have well written material, you intuitively and instantly immerse yourself into the part and make smart choices." This acknowledgment began to lead me to understand that perhaps film and television acting was not for me. Yet, while I slowly resolved to do something else in the business, another challenge presented itself.

My commercial agent was frustrated that I wasn't getting cast in many of the parts he sent me out to read for. The problem, according to the casting agent, was my look. In California at the time, if they wanted a Caucasian for the part, it was often a light-skinned, blond-haired actor they were after. Naturally, I had dark hair and olive pigmented skin. The agent tried a different, albeit unethical, tactic and sent me out a couple of times to audition for commercials produced for the Hispanic community. Forget the fact that I didn't speak the language, but when a darker complexioned Caucasian is placed in a room with Hispanic actors, he looks comparatively white.

Attempting to further my education, I took a class on acting for television commercials, and learned a practice that I still use, and teach, others today. When people take professional photos, they can often have a blank look. They're not focusing on the lens, or if they are they have a nervous, "deer in the headlights" look. It's for important reasons they're taking these photos, nerves come with that territory. What I learned when talking to a camera applied when being behind it as well. The secret to coming across as genuine was to imagine the lens as someone specific. If you are to look happy, then imagine the person as someone you love. In today's time, when everyone is using computer rooms for meetings, I can apply this learning. Pretending to talk to one specific person when looking at a lens, you are seen as inclusive to everyone watching. With most business meetings being on digital platforms, this practice continues to serve me well.

Hands down, the best acting lesson I've learned took place in a film performance workshop that I joined for a brief period called The Jim Best Acting Workshop. Mr. Best played many parts over the course of his career, including appearances in *The Andy Griffith Show* (1960-1968) and a recurring role as "Sheriff Rosco Coltrane" in the series *The Dukes of Hazzard* (1979-1985). While Mr. Best did not teach the class, one night our coach put our session on hold and us that he was coming in that night to help another actor, a stuntman named Dar Robinson, prepare for a big audition. Robinson was up for a part in a Burt Reynolds starrer called *Stick* (1985). He was carefully preparing to read for the part of a villain, a role where if he were cast, would have to perform a high falling stunt off a building.

While many other classmates looked away, engaged in conversation, I did what I grew up doing at home. I intently watched and listened to the instruction that Mr. Best gave to Robinson. "Don't blink. Especially when you're a bad guy, don't blink." He threw out a threatening line and spoke it twice, showing the difference. Once he said it without blinking, and once he said it blinking his eyes halfway through. The difference between the almost identical performances was small, but noticeable. Robinson got the part, and now when I watch a film, I pay extra attention to the villain. I'll notice the subtle difference in the performances and if an actor blinks or not. Now you will too, and I believe that you will also notice that the better actors are the ones who either do not blink or do so with intention. Regardless, it feels like with a blink of an eye, our family had gone from the top of the business to the middle.

Chapter 6

Doing What They Did When They Could

By the late '70s, we had moved to the smaller house on Lemp Avenue. A move is tough enough for any family, but this one was memorable for many reasons. We moved on April 19, 1977, my mother's 40th birthday. It was also the final day of shooting of the first *Father Knows Best Reunion* special and the first day of filming for the television movie that would become her next series, *Mulligan's Stew*! It is a date my mother remembers for all of these reasons and one that she told me recently, "I'll never forget." A tough move, certainly, yet into a wonderful neighborhood.

In that same neighborhood lived a couple of silent film folk, who as luck would have it, lived in the same apartment my grandmother did. Harvey Perry was a famous stuntman, as was Paul Malvern who later became a producer. Malvern loved to tell the story about the time he was preparing to execute a stunt in place of silent movie leading man, Douglas Fairbanks Sr., in *Robin Hood* (1922). The stunt had the main character getting into a catapult and upon release being thrust to the top level of a castle. When he was in the actor's wardrobe, the director pointed to the catapult and told him that he was ready to shoot the scene. Malvern refused since he had not been involved in the development of the stunt itself and wanted to be sure he wouldn't be injured or killed during the action.

The director dismissed his concerns and assured him that others had worked it out scientifically and it was all perfectly calibrated. Malvern stubbornly insisted on a test. The director acquiesced and following his instructions, had a large sack of sugar that weighed exactly as much as Malvern placed into the catapult. Everyone stood back and, as the catapult was released, watched the sack of sugar as it flew way above and behind the castle. In simultaneous realization, they knew if Malvern had gone in place of this test, he would have been killed. "So much for your calculations," Malvern remarked as he reworked the device so the stunt was eventually performed safely and successfully. This story reminds me to be an active participant in my own life story, and not just a spectator.

Whether it was through the opportunity of living at the time that I did, my parents' connections, or the area I resided, I'm delighted to have experienced many life and show biz lessons, from some of the most unappreciated masters of their craft. The Lemp Avenue period was wonderful. From my point of view, it was as if we moved into a Classic Television show's neighborhood. Our neighbors were nice, approachable, and looked out for one another. These folks included families who we're still close with-- the Diamonds, the Rameys, and we actually had the Joneses living across the street! Mom continued doing what she did best; auditioning and working when the offers came by.

It was after our Lemp Ave. move that my mom's agent, with her agreement, did a push to get her into television commercials. Because of the frequency of these mini productions, she auditioned with a greater frequency than she had for television, however, that meant increased rejection when she did not get a part. Her last commercial was the one on which she was cast in this period, for a cold medicine. It only aired once, from what I remembered, and it was a stop motion film shot of my mom sneezing. For her, it was a declarative turning point in her career. During the shoot for that product, her day consisted of sneezing over, and over, and over. She was directed to sneeze one way and then another. Long sneezes, short sneezes, heavy sneezes, light sneezes. "While doing so," she recalled to me, "I thought of all the nice work I'd done in the past and decided, 'That's it!'"

Thankfully, she was able to continue to find work in television and do what she loved. Whether it was *The Love Boat, Fantasy Island, Mork & Mindy* (1978-1982), *S.W.A.T.* (1975-1976), *Police*

Story, or more, she worked fairly steadily. As many know, fame is fleeting; but if one is lucky, there is always an audience. I knew things were different when clarifying my mother's work became challenging. For a good decade or two, I merely had to say, "She played Betty on *Father Knows Best.*" A decade or so later, I received the more regular response of, "She played who on what?" For a long while people were happy when I named a show they recognized. As time has gone on, and people become more inclined to watch Classic Television, I have been able to hit the highlights – if they are an *Andy Griffith Show*, *Star Trek: The Original Series*, or *The Odd Couple* fan, I have them covered. Thankfully, the late Garry Marshall's *Pretty Woman* has me covered. When I describe her as the "nice sales lady" I even get young folks recognizing her.

There were so many roles for her. For me, there was a special responsibility that afforded me an opportunity to watch her craft her characters.

Script Buddy

Memories I will always cherish are the times, beginning in my pre-teen years and continuing into young adulthood while I lived at home, when I helped my mom memorize her lines. After running through her pages a few times, she would then ask me to run lines with her, testing her memory and giving her a chance to work through different takes and actions. I would sit across from her and read every other character's dialogue as she would recite her own. Before we began, she would instruct me on specifics; how exact she wanted or needed lines to be, whether the words had to be exact or if it was okay to change it a little. I learned to ask if she wanted me to tell her what she missed after we completed the run-through or during. So much of acting is trial and error. Once we had figured out all the parameters, we would read.

Over the years, I have read the lines in place of Felix and Oscar from *The Odd Couple*, cast members from *Happy Days*, and many others. My mother always complimented me on this and though my brothers might have tried as well, she liked my style. As a budding fellow actor, I knew that it was not my time to perform, but to deliver lines in an authentic, non-theatrical manner, in ways that allowed her to respond. She taught me that our goal in these moments was not about acting, but about memorization. This practice of knowing her lines, of having them down, allowed her emotional attachment to the words to be fresh when interacting with others in the official filming. Once an actor has their lines down, they can authentically add in emotion and not have to struggle dividing attention between committing fully in heart and remembering what to actually say. The basis for acting is first knowing the lines. Not saying I'm special, but of her four sons, I was her go-to for this kind of preparation.

During pre-production for *The Father Knows Best Reunion Special,* my mother shared with Jane Wyatt what a help I was to her in memorizing lines. Jane was ecstatic and replied, "I need someone to do that. Do you think you could bring Peter to the stage and have your son run my lines with me?" My mother asked me, and I was so excited; I was going to help at least two cast members with their lines. Alas, that experience was denied to me by the title character, who I guess in fact, did know best.

The first day of work on the set for the cast was not a pleasant one. In short, Robert Young was not happy with the cast bringing family members to the set. Mr. Young, who publicly battled his own demons, was strictly a professional. That word can mean different things to different people. He was one of those men who, like my father, focused on producing a product. Unlike my father, however, Mr. Young's version of on-sct professionalism apparently did not include any sense of fun or personal time. He openly let Lauren Chapin know that her daughter was not welcome on the set, and it was his stance and declarations that prevented me from ever visiting a *Father Knows Best Reunion* filming. "Well, you are definitely *not* going to the set with me tomorrow," was unfortunately my mother's never-changing statement.

Still, I loved television, and I loved the fact that my parents wore the coattails that I could ride to get behind the scenes. Though I never got to go on a *Father Knows Best Reunion* set, I did get to meet all of the cast, (except Mr. Young, of course) and I am personally not sorry for the latter, but I do know that my mother loved and respected him very much, despite his on-set presence and style of "professionalism."

Unfortunately for me, I did not always take my mother up on helping her. Production sets can get lonely, especially if you are working only one day. Such was the case when Garry Marshall cast her in a movie. I was living on my own, but she reached out to me, and said "I am working on a movie, and we are filming on Sunday. The production has closed off Rodeo Drive in Beverly Hills for the day, I am sure I will be sitting around a lot, and would love you to keep me company, and help me run through my lines." Sundays were often the only day I got any rest, so I was reticent, but asked who was in the scene with her? She replied, just the lead actress, some woman, I cannot remember her name at the moment, she was just in a film called *Mystic Pizza*." Having not seen the movie, I had no idea who my mom was talking about. And that led me to miss my chance to hang out on the set of the movie my mom worked on, *Pretty Woman*, and meet Julia Roberts! Still, there were the times when I went with her to sets. However, when she was not filming in front of a live audience, there was one rule to follow I learned early on, and when I did not follow the directive, oh was it noticeable.

When Filming, Stay Out of Mom's Eyeline, and Other Lessons

Interactions with my mother on sets was limited because she, like any good actor, is there to focus on her part and she does so admirably. More than anything else, I believe that watching her taught me a good work ethic; show up early, be as ready as you can be, be flexible, and do what you are there to do. It was a rare treat to see my mother act. I can't think, except for *The Flying Nun* and the short-lived series *Mulligan's Stew* (1977), that I ever saw my mother both rehearse and film a part. If I was on set, there was only one rule that I respected. Or at least tried to. "Please stay out of my range of sight so I cannot see you. It pulls me out of character." So, I would find places away from the set. In the shadows, I would watch from there. However, there was one occasion that my usual hiding didn't work. It was sometime in the 1980s, as cable was taking off, and we were on the soundstage for a network that was solely devoted to selling items, much like QVC and other shopping channels today. For some reason, my mother needed me to pick her up from the studio when her work concluded around noon.

As I was headed onto the stage, I remember seeing the sign that indicated they were always live and always filming, and to be quiet and careful when going around the set. It was an impressive operation. In one location, there was a news desk sort of operation when the anchor would make an announcement or help segue from one selling segment to the next. Surrounding the stage were different set-like cubicles, one next to the other. In one was a celebrity being prepped for their pitching of a new product. In another was a man known as "Body by Jake," getting ready for his segment which followed my mother's. And there, live in her section with three cameras in front filming from different angles, was my mother with the pitch person, talking about how remarkable this particular vacuum cleaner was. I wasn't too close to the set, and certainly in the shadows, so I thought that I was okay. But oh man, was I wrong.

There was a teleprompter on the set that had the various selling points about the product that my mother was supposed to keep bringing up, and it turned out that I was standing in such a way that as she looked at it, my face was what she saw above it. That was bad enough, but what happened next made it a bit worse for both of us. My mother, with a bit of mother to son, "you should know better" annoyance on her face, waved her hand as my signal to get out of her sightline. Instead, the co-host on the set noticed the gesture and asked, "Elinor, who are you waving to out there?"

My mother is a great actress, and like the best of them, could think on her feet. So, when in doubt, tell the truth. "Oh!" she said in her Elinor/Betty Anderson voice, "It's my son, Peter!" Well, all of the camera operators, sound technicians, and set crew had earphones on to receive direction, which all undoubtedly at that moment, were transitioned to me. And there I was, by myself, the set of lights above me now shining me in the spotlight. Cameras flashing that red recording light, I knew I was now on live television. The host continued. "Well, Peter, are you here visiting your mother? How do you like the house now that she uses the 'such and such' vacuum cleaner?" I muttered something and thankfully I was a boring enough subject that the lights over me faded, and the cameras quickly went back to their business at hand. True professional that she was, my mother picked right up and went with it. "Well, you know with four boys in the home, one is always cleaning, and let me tell you this product..."

When I began to get some on camera work as an actor, it was my mother who first gave me good advice about on-set etiquette. Her guidance became useful when, for a brief period, I acted on television. Though regrettably we never worked together, we have been a part of a few of the same shows, such as *Days of Our Lives* (1965-). When she co-starred in an episode of *Friends* in the first season, I went on to work in the production office for the next two.

Oftentimes, she was predictably cast as a new, age-appropriate version of her *Father Knows Best* character, Betty Anderson. When opportunities came for her to play against character, she could delve more into her acting craft. It was on *Days of our Lives*, and other celebrity-filled shows like *The Love Boat* or *Fantasy Island* (1977-1984), where she was cast as darker characters. In a conversation I once had with Gavin MacLeod, who not only played Captain Stubing on *The Love Boat*, but also performed dinner theater with my mother, he commented on what a great actress she truly was. "If they would only give her better parts!" he said. I agree. Thankfully, *Days of Our*

Lives gave her that opportunity. It was her experience on that set I got to share with her, as I began to be cast in various small roles on the show.

On *Days of our Lives,* I played "under five" roles. This is a union designation for pay and means that your character has under five lines (or fewer than sixty words). Sometimes the part would have those fifty-nine words allotted, and others were one-liners, like, "Yes, Doctor!" I have portrayed everything from a policeman who presented smoking remnants of a time machine to the police captain to a bell boy delivering champagne to the couple in the hotel. Often, as was the case when I played an EMT or a reporter, my two-word line was lost in the other dialogue of the scene.

Days of Our Lives was, even without my mother's etiquette training, an eye-opening experience. The episode filmed over the course of a day and is done very carefully. First is the stage blocking, then next a quick run-through for the cameras, then the filming. When I was first going to work on the show, my mother gave me sage advice for the actor in a very small role. The epitome of her advice was always kindness. "Be nice to everyone, and never complain, because you never know who you may be talking to or to whom they might be related." She also warned me to, "Be careful of what you say to and about anyone, anywhere on a set. You never know when a nearby microphone is 'live'. If you want to be critical about someone or something, just keep it to yourself!" The takeaway: on a film set, there are eyes and ears everywhere. She'd always mention how she'd been convinced on a soap opera set that even the common room, where the day actors could go to hang out, study their lines, chat or rest, had a hidden microphone. One day a fellow actor had been griping about one thing or another while in the space, and next thing she knew, he was replaced. While she admits now there probably wasn't a hidden anything and it was paranoia, her cautionary tale still served me well.

I was cast as a reporter on the show, with three other "under five" actors also cast as reporters. As we sat together waiting for direction,

I noticed one particular woman. Though it was only 6:00 am, she already had her hair up in curlers, but was still dressed down in sweats with no make-up. All the while, she complained. I was in my mid to late 20s at this point, and between the rare acting gigs, I was also working in Television Commercial and Music Video Production. I often dealt with talent, including the extras who complained. While this fellow actor continued on about the competency of the director, the temperature in the studio, and more, there was a part of me that wanted to "school" her. I wanted to let her know that the set was especially cold now because later when the cameras and lights were on, they would generate oppressive heat. I even understood why our call time was so early, and I wanted to show off my knowledge and true understanding of sets. However, I felt like Obi Wan Kenobi's voice echoing in Luke Skywalkers head, my mother's wisdom reigned. So, I stayed quiet.

Turns out, my mother knew best (see what I did there)! When I returned to the scene later in the morning for the run-through with the cameras, I realized the woman was not some under-five day player but was actually one of the stars of the show-- a woman to whom my brother James and I delivered papers to back when we had a route. Had I inadvertently "schooled" one of the stars of the show, it would not have ended well for me. (I would like to point out that this moment proves, that yes, I can keep my mouth shut at times when it needs to stay that way).

As my mother continued to work, Dad's career rebounded, due to a nostalgia phase that began in the early 1980s.

Redemption: Everything Old is New Again

As I was earning my master class in what it takes to be an actor in Hollywood in the early 1980s, my parents were doing their best to redefine their place in the industry. Thankfully, as fickle as show business is, it can also be joyfully unpredictable; and before he died in 1991, Dad would have one more go-round at displaying his strengths.

A main reason networks no longer looked to produce shows like the ones my father made was because there was an audience craving for edgy. Programs like *Soap* (1977-1981), or *All in the Family* began to thrive. Regardless, if my father was given the opportunity to adjust his style or not, he wouldn't forgo that formula he swore by, the one that appealed to families as a whole, and not just to specific age segments. But then it happened. *The Cosby Show* (1984-1992) became a big hit, with a premise that hearkened back to the classic shows of old. Move over *Father Knows Best, The Adventures of Ozzie & Harriet* (1952-1966), *Hazel, The Donna Reed* Show (1958-1966), and *Leave It to Beaver*, there was a new family in television: the Huxtables.

Suddenly, the formula from the good old days of Harry Ackerman shows was desirable, and my dad was able to get in one last addition to his resume. Oftentimes, he returned to the character of Gidget. After the show with Sally Field, he produced a couple of *Gidget* TV movies, and now by the middle of the '80s, he was able to bring the character back to the airwaves again.

The TV movie *Gidget's Summer Reunion* (1985) is what led to the two-season syndicated series, *The New Gidget*. This was also where my desire to be an actor began to be realized. Shortly after I appeared in both the *Gidget* movie and subsequent series, it was the latter where I received my first taste of "behind the scenes" life, which led to me working for people in production end for a while.

The acting was actually unplanned. I helped the casting department for the movie because one of the actors was unavailable to read with the actresses trying out for the part of Gidget's niece. So, Dad sent me in. I read the part of the nerdy bookworm teen along with the late Dana Plato from *Diff'rent Strokes* (1978-1986) and Khrystyne Haje from *The Head of the Class* (1986-1991). At one point, an executive leaned over to my dad and seriously considered casting me, and while it's a very nice compliment, the talented David Knell was marvelous.

Casting can be very odd and ever-changing. Allison Barron was originally cast in the role of the niece, who, when the show went to series, was recast with Sydney Penny—a fine actress who was then making a name for herself in Clint Eastwood's film *Pale Rider* (1985) and was quite the rising star. Since she looked more like she would be related to Caryn Richman, who played Gidget, that may have played a part in the movie vs. TV show casting change.

Joining Richman to head the cast was Dean Butler. At the time, Richman and I were in the same acting class together. Since I was both beginning to realize that acting was not a career for me and that she was nervous I'd report all her mix-ups or bad days with my dad, I stopped attending that class so my friend could be at ease. She continued with that acting coach, and it showed. She is not only a marvelous actress, but she seriously stepped it up and made a great Gidget!

In remembering that time of her life, Caryn told me, "I never dreamed that I would play Gidget. I grew up on the East Coast, but when I moved to Los Angeles to try acting out there, I always found the Malibu culture exciting. Partly because I grew up watching *Gidget* and *The Flying Nun*!" "I remember my final audition," she continued, "Actresses, one at a time of course, were asked to perform a monologue." In referring to herself, she said, "For a young actress, a conference table full of television and network executives was not an easy audience. I remember your dad in that casting session. When I looked over at him, he had a literal twinkle in his eyes. That show of confidence anchored me. Your dad grounded me with a simple smile that calmed my nervousness."

Caryn loved that working for my dad connected her to Classic Television. "I went to your home to do a photoshoot with your dad. Until then, I didn't know his rich history. In those days in Hollywood, it was just 'TV,' there was no 'Classic TV' yet."

Larry Mollin, a writer-producer on my dad's syndicated *The New Gidget* series, which aired in the middle 1980s, shared, "We filmed five episodes at a time; one full day at the beach to shoot that many episodes worth of material. Every day (on set or on location) he was present. He was thrilled to talk to the cast and crew, and they were with him (in the spirit of creating the show)." Mollin further recalls, "If he ever had to have words with someone; as the Executive Producer, he took them aside; he never publicly embarrassed anyone." That is the same way Dad would talk to us as his sons. Things were handled privately and not embarrassingly in front of others.

In regard to Field's autobiography presenting Harry as a mystery man, Mollin commented, "Harry was never mysterious. He was a father or grandfather type; not a threatening guy!" Even a favorite mystery author of our family, John D. MacDonald, was a big fan of Harry. Mr. MacDonald and my dad became pen pals when they tried to bring the author's Travis McGee character to television, but it was a project that sadly never came together. My mother came the closest to working with the author when she was cast and co-starred in *Condominium* (1980), a television miniseries based on a later novel by the author. According to Macdonald's biographer, "MacDonald liked Ackerman, something he never felt for producers." "He is that rare bird out there, a man who actually reads books," [MacDonald] wrote to [his friend] Max Wilkinson (p. 153)."[4]

These written characteristics of Harry represent the patriarch of my family whom I knew, and whom I saw represented in his workplaces as well. Dean Butler, who played Almanzo on the *Little House on the Prairie* (1974-1983), worked on the last Harry Ackerman series, *The New Gidget*, as the title character's long-time love and now husband Jeff "Moondoggie" Griffin. In a personal conversation with me when my dad was still alive, Butler said, "You know, your dad is the best producer, and here is why; he listens!" In a time when he was unhappy with a director's choice for his character, he made an appointment with Harry to discuss it. "He

------

4   The Red Hot Typewriter: The Life of John D. MacDonald, Hugh Merrill, Thomas Dunne Books: St. Martin's Minotaur, New York, 2000, p. 153

heard me out. He listened to what I had to say, and you could see that he actually took in my concerns and was considering what to do with them." With a laugh he added, "Nothing changed, mind you, but I really know that he took what I brought to him to heart and considered what I brought to him."

Producer Larry Mollin also remembers *The New Gidget* period as the unique opportunity it was in the mid-1980s to see classic Hollywood television through Harry and others. It was that positive impact that new Hollywood unfolded during that period. "Harry was one of TV's pioneers," Mollin reminisced. "He came from a time when the process was slower. One would film one day, watch dailies the next, and it forced the department heads, writers, and executives to always be in the same room together. But by the 1980s, video had become the norm." Mollin refers to the culture change where what was just filmed did not need to be developed. It could be watched on set at the moment of production. People no longer needed to sit in the same space and watch or edit feedback together. Mollin stated, for better or worse, "it made a completely different world."

Yet in that different world was a mash-up of cultures that would never be seen again. Mollin shared with me how, "it was a wonderful time. People like Harry were older and still around. He hired many others (his contemporaries) for crew or acting roles. Carroll Pratt was the 'laugh track guy.' Harry knew just what the product needed." In telling a story about editing an episode where laughs needed to be added, he recalled how, "Carroll would look to Harry. Harry would mimic the kind of laugh, chuckle or guffaw he wanted, and Carroll would put that particular track to the section of the show. He (Harry) knew where the laughs would be. He did not have to find it; it was totally just natural."

As I mentioned earlier, I was cast in the TV movie that began the series, *Gidget's Summer Reunion*, as one of three surfers, alongside actors Vince Van Patten and Brad Zutaut. I can remember beginning the movie with my first line as the three of us emerged from the surf– "Hey, check this out!" My character's final shot was a fight scene on the beach, and I had so much fun filming in that role. However, it's not exactly a "day at the beach" when you film at the beach, in the water, on a gorgeous sunny day in March, when the water is FREEZING!

The most fun was the cast. I looked forward to each day, cold weather or not, heading to the beach to hang out with these people. During a break in filming, Vince Van Patten and I drove in his vintage Mustang down Pacific Coast Highway, with the bright sun cascading down upon us. Vince and I shared a laugh and reminisced about how ten years earlier, while I was at some celebrity-filled event with my parents, I was able to secure a young Van Patten autograph after running into him in the men's room. Sharing memories past brought us into the then present– a true *California Dreamin'* moment as we drove down PCH! It was one of those times that felt and looked like a true Hollywood experience.

Vince comes from a talented and wonderful family. I almost discovered the hard way how close-knit they are. A week or so after my beach filming, I was with friends dining at a favorite restaurant of mine, Casa Vega, on Ventura Boulevard in Studio City. I had been sharing my tales on the set and included my time motoring with Vince. Apparently, I said his name just loud enough. A guy sitting behind me excused himself from his table, and the next thing I knew this hulking fellow was standing above ours and staring me down… hard. He said, "I heard you saying something about Vince Van Patten. I'm his older brother. You want to tell me what you said and maybe go outside and talk about it?" Thankfully, I only had good things to say about Vince and shared the story with his brother who softened, shook my hand, and returned to his table.

When I was in my 20s, I had the pleasure to act in a television movie executive produced by my dad, which later became the syndicated series *The New Gidget* (1986-1988). In the telefilm, *Gidget's Summer Reunion* (1985), I played Darryl, one of the two mean surfer buddies, along with actor Brad Zutaut, to the main character played by Vince Van Patten. We were the beach trio holding our beach against Gidget and her old timer pals who wanted to come back.

For the week I worked on the project, we filmed in Paradise Cove in Malibu, California, where many shows including *The Rockford Files* (1974-1980) were filmed. During this time, I experienced the same professional, yet relaxed, comradery between the cast and crew. That is to say, a typical experience with a Harry Ackerman Production. One morning, though, a young temporary makeup artist hired for the day came into our make-up trailer as one of our young co-stars left for set. While being unable to find a brush she was certain she brought with her, she grudgingly spoke, "If that bitch took it, she had better bring it back." After frustratingly searching and being unsuccessful, she stepped out of the trailer. As soon as she was out of earshot, the head of the production's department said to his staff member who was applying my makeup, "Call the union and let them know we do not want her back, and that they should send us someone else." This production department head did what my dad would have. He didn't have the patience for attitude or comments like that, and this kind of demeanor is what helps keep and create a family set.

It was here, as an adult, that I saw how the production system of one of my dad's shows operated as a family. I further appeared as various characters in three episodes of the show over its two-year run. By the last one, I realized what a horrible film actor I was (truly). The character they gave me was something that I just could not get into, and I did not do well. I don't believe that I even watched it and hope never to do so. By that time, I discovered my innate love of the production end, and was already leaning towards that, which I'm sure the public was grateful for. Just had happened when I was a pre-teen on the set of The Paul Lynde Show, an opportunity arose for me to have a two-week front row center learning lab at watching my dad and others at work, and I took it.

Learning Television Production

The opportunity to learn on the set of *The New Gidget* happened on both sides of the camera. First, from when I was cast in the series, and second when I became my dad's driver for two weeks.

As an actor, I was in a scene with a few other actors, including one of the show's regulars, William Schallert. He was a veteran of the medium and an immensely talented actor who, like my mother, seemed to appear in every television series over the course of his long life. In the middle of the 1980s, he was cast as Gidget's father in the TV movie and series, *The New Gidget*, executive produced by my dad (on which I acted a few times). I was in this particular scene with Mr. Schallert and a couple of other actors, one of whom was a young man who followed the script and said his line. Once the scene was over and the actor walked away, Schallert turned to me and said with some frustration in his voice, "he is not finding the comedy in the line. The laugh is there, if only he will help it out." He then repeated the kid's line to me, which included a beat at the right moment and a verbal highlighting of the final words which included wordplay on "carbohydrates." "But Dad, he *conned* me…with *carbos*!" Schallert showed me how a seemingly innocent line could become something greater.

At the time of filming for *The New Gidget*, my dad had undergone minor surgery. He was unable to drive, and asked if I would take two weeks off of my job as a server at the Hamburger Hamlet restaurant in Sherman Oaks to drive him to his studio appointments. It was then, as an adult, that I witnessed my dad in vocational action. Yes, I sat with him in front of the television over the years watching shows, getting a sense of how to build a joke, and learning what made something funny or not. I even had a taste when I sat for most of the week during *The Paul Lynde Show* and observed him interacting with the crew and actors, listening to them, and asking questions, etc. However, this was a different perspective.

I heard an ear-opener, (yes, you read that correctly), at one casting session. It was being held in an empty office that was adjacent to my dad's at Warner Bros. television. Sally Powers, who was the series casting director, brought in about five men who were called back for a second audition, this time for my dad and the other writers and producers like George Zateslo and Larry Mollin. It was inappropriate for me to be present for the sessions, so I left for dad's office, and sat behind his desk. As the actors were brought in from the hallway, they made a beeline for the adjacent room, and when the door closed, I listened.

After introductions and questions, the actor would read, then perhaps be given some additional direction, and read again. At the end, the actor was thanked by the casting group as he left, and soon the next prospective performer was escorted into the room. The part that they were casting was that of a high school football coach. His lines were written something like, "All right, Jones, get down and give me twenty! Oh, don't you like that? Well, maybe forty will make you feel better!" I had no doubt who would get the part. Another clue to being a good actor: it's not merely about your look and ability to read the lines correctly but being able to deliver them believably. All the men who came in looked like football coaches, at least the television version of one, but there was only one who sounded like a football coach. No joke, when he read off, "Give me twenty!" I almost hit the floor and began doing push-ups. Later, while driving Dad to the editing bay off-site, I told him who I bet got the part. "How did you know?" he asked. When I told him, he reiterated the same point. That actor was the only one who was a believable football coach.

For two weeks I listened to casting, observed editing, and more. During editing sessions one day, I met the aforementioned Caroll Pratt, master of the laugh track. "You want to hear your mom's bedroom door slamming on *Father Knows Best*?" He pushed a couple buttons, and I heard the "slam!" "Here was the chuckle we would use to augment the laughs on *I Love Lucy*," and like an old familiar song, I heard invisible people giggling. He knew his sound board, and it was apparent that, like my dad, he loved his job and coveted his unique connection to Classic Television history.

As an experiential learner, it was while observing Dad as he interacted with others that I understood on a deeper level his personal creed: "I will never retire, I love what I do too much." On a production, he surrounded himself not only with the best-skilled people but with good-natured ones. Crew and production personnel were the type who you didn't mind going to see every day. They carried out their work professionally and were approachable and friendly. For me, this camaraderie throughout the crew was the magic of a Harry Ackerman show. It was a healthy system where people came to do a job but worked as a family. I got it. Those two weeks were the final piece of my completing my firm decision to go into production instead of acting.

This two-week education nudged me onto the road of my television, commercial, and music video production career. During this time, I was also a few months away from getting married, so professionally and personally, it felt as if all the pieces of my life were coming together. There, with my newest vocation, my life began to take a new path. The first stage of that new walk meant that it was time to leave the nest of my parents' home, in which I had become too comfortable.

He's Leaving Home!

Yes, though second in line of the four boys who lived with our parents, I became the last bird to leave the next. The first was Brian, then James when he went into the Coast Guard, and not long after that was baby brother, Chris. I was that one child who knew a good thing when he had it. While I was going to school, working as a waiter, and thinking about becoming a professional actor, living with my parents was, as I look back, a frustration to them who probably wanted an empty nest. However, I was selfishly oblivious in my comfort with my decisions. When I was about a year away from my decision to move from acting into production, my parents decided that it was time for me to leave their nest. The home I lived in as a teenager, through high school and junior college, was no longer mine to stay in. They realized that this bird needed a not-so-gentle shove. So, one Monday afternoon while I was waiting tables, I was surprised to find my mom and dad sitting in my section. They enjoyed a snack along with some beverages, and while it was slow, they took the opportunity to engage me in a brief conversation when I came over.

My mother asked me, "Do you have any plans after your shift ends this afternoon?" I shook my head and she said, "Your father and I were out today, and we came across a lovely little apartment nearby. It's so cute, so perfect for someone like you, and very affordable." I confirmed the plan already was in motion when I showed up at the furnished apartment to find the manager with a rental agreement and pen, ready for my signature. After I looked around the unit, I agreed that it was nice, and the rent was extremely reasonable. My dad, ever the businessman, knew how to close a sale. He took me aside and said, "Peter, I don't want you to feel abandoned," and with those words gave me a handshake promise of a year's allowance to help with the cost of the rental. Of course, I signed the paper and that was how I found myself finally living on my own.

What I remember most about that important time was the promise that my mother gave me. "This will be good for you, but honey, don't worry. If it doesn't work out, your room at home will always be available." That assurance may have been her intention at the moment, but I kid you not, when I stopped by their house a few weeks later and looked in my old bedroom, I saw that the space had been transformed into an entertainment center. With a quiet laugh, I knew then for sure what I assumed after I moved out: there would be no going home again! Moving out of their home was a good change. It was the right change. The alteration of my old bedroom space made for good memories later on. It was in that entertainment room where my dad and I hung out, watched movies together, and had deep conversations about the films we loved dearly. Remembering those times reassured me that before he died, I received quality and intimate time with my dad.

On my own in the mid-1980s allowed my life, both professional and personal, to come together. As to the latter, my wife Marie, with whom I've been married since 1987, and I met a few years before while I was waiting tables, still working to become an actor. On the great debate around if love at first sight truly exists, I weigh in on the affirmative. It was a Sunday evening, and I was waiting to clock into my shift. Lined up with other servers doing the same, we waited for the clock to hit the hour. I was talking with my co-worker Joanie, who had gone with me to see a play a few nights before, and this was the first time we were able to talk about it afterwards. As we carried on, my eyes suddenly caught the sight of a young woman at the front of our restaurant. She was in the process of seating a group of people, and I interrupted Joanie, asking her if she knew who that was. She replied, "Oh, her name is Marie, she's the new hostess who started yesterday." I tell no lie. From that first moment, I knew Marie was the one.

Marie was and always will be my one. She was immediately accepted as a member of my family. My mother, having raised four boys, took any opportunity to welcome a daughter figure into the family. Dad always respected his son's choices in spouses, and like Mom, readily included them as a part of the family. As life progressed, my siblings and I all married, and eventually all had children, giving my parents the coveted and loving roles of grandparents.

Whether it was truly love at first sight, or something else, Marie has shared in my life's adventures. She was there when, almost immediately following our marriage, I transitioned from pursuing acting as a career and began working in production for television commercials and music videos. It was during the next five years that we began a family with the birth of our son Harry in 1991, and daughter Amy in 1994. By the time Amy was born, I had transitioned even further in my career, working in television production at Warner Bros. Television in various departments and on shows. Little did I know that within the next decade, I would be headed to graduate school to engage in a whole new career.

During my job transitions, and between her pregnancies, Marie was the one who kept constant work. She remained in the food and beverage industry, later becoming a sommelier, or wine expert, which is what she still does to this day, alongside managing a restaurant. It's felt like the trajectory of our life has always been predicated on the notion, "do what you love, and the rest will fall into place." This was advice given to me first and foremost by my mother. She didn't want me to be an actor, as she knew how tough it was. This is why she never pushed me into it, and was completely fine, probably relieved even, when my older brother declined the offer to play a friend for Opie on *The Andy Griffith Show*. When she noted that I was serious in desiring to pursue acting after graduating from high school, she supported me fully, but asked me to promise her that if I found something I loved doing more than performing, I'd do that. And I did. Staying consistent in choosing what we love has kept life interesting and fulfilling for both Marie and for me.

Yet, no matter what one does, we all tend to meet life on life's terms, and it was no different for my parents. After Marie and I were married, *The New Gidget* continued for one more season and then wasn't renewed. It aired only two seasons and may never be seen in re-runs due to the more restrictive music licensing of the day. As Marie and I moved deeper into marriage, and as I became a father, I was even less involved in my parents' careers than before. Mom continued to actively perform, but my dad's life literally and professionally began winding down.

First Vocational Shift

It all came together. Those couple of weeks maneuvering my dad to his production responsibilities and my getting married made me realize that it was time to shift into the production end of the business. About one week after returning from our honeymoon, I took a leap of faith and quit my restaurant gig, fully prepared to dive into a new role working as a freelance production assistant. I began with television commercials. In the late 1980s, a PA could be placed in the office, farmed out to various departments on a film set, be assigned to drive trucks, or run various errands, such as picking up more film or driving other crew members to where they needed to be. I worked steadily for five years freelancing from one job to the next, each lasting as little as one day to a week or more. Each job gave me new contacts, and thus the work kept coming. So did the miracles, as I worked with many stars and celebrities.

I was working at a small studio in Hollywood on another commercial starring film actor Anthony Perkins. One day, I returned from an off the lot errand and encountered Perkins casually standing outside of the soundstage. After a brief conversation, I took out my production book, which included the one-page script for the commercial which paid homage to the Hitchcock film *Psycho* and the others in the series that he starred in and once directed and asked him to sign it. He did, while asking me what my interest was in obtaining it? Was I a film fan, a Hitchcock aficionado? I admitted that I merely appreciated him and his work and wanted the souvenir.

Later that same week, I experienced when my dad's world and mine intersected. This time, for the same breakfast cereal where we used Anthony Perkins. This time we filmed with the now grown-up members of the Leave It To Beaver Cast, Barbara Billingsley, who played the mother and Jerry Mathers (Beaver). One day during the production, I was hanging out with them in the motor home that served as their dressing room and rest area. My dad had executive produced the first season of the show, and they remembered him. Jerry, in fact, said some really nice things about my dad, and how he helped him adjust to the production life.

I was a production assistant on lots of celebrity commercials, working with Arnold Schwarzenegger, and Los Angeles Dodgers' baseball manager, Tommy Lasorda, to name a few. However, when I am asked, "Who is the most famous person you ever worked with?" Two people come to mind, Burt Lancaster, and Chuck Yeager.

I worked with Mr. Lancaster at a later time in his life when he was not very happy. Older, he was almost forced into retirement after being denied by a studio insurance company to work on a movie called *The Old Gringo*. Whether that is what led him to accepting the part of a celebrity spokesman for senior health care (not for the company who denied his movie work), I do not know. However, he carried himself with a certain dignity. I do not know enough about the man to know if that was just his way, or if he was keeping his ego lifted despite working on a television commercial. I saw the dignity in action the one day he worked with us on set. I was sent to get him from the motor home in which he rested, and on the way to the set, just after we entered the interior of the stage, his foot hit the end of a long metal device causing him to stumble slightly. It was a folded in piece of camera track, used when a camera had to move. I was behind Mr. Lancaster when his foot hit the track and noticed that it was where it was supposed to be, nestled well within the painted red lines around it. Perhaps he missed it because he had just stepped from a well-lit trailer onto a darker outer part of the stage and his eyes had not adjusted. Yet, after regaining his footing, he stopped, leaned over, and with one hand picked up that heavy piece and moved it further inward before placing it down. It was his silent, dignified way of suggesting the track was at fault. I did not correct him. This was a good thing because what happened next might have gotten me fired.

Because Burt Lancaster was only available for one day of filming, the production had to get ready the day before, so that after the lights and the camera were ready we could go right to filming. On that pre-production day, I was on the set when the fellow who was running the tele-prompter wanted to be sure the device was working. So, the actor did not have to memorize the text, the words he needed to say flowed into view on a see-through screen in front of the camera's lens, so that the actor could read his lines as he spoke into the camera lens, looking like he was speaking to the viewer. The technician asked if I would be so kind as to stand in Burt's place and read the text. Asking a former actor to stand in front of a camera was no problem, especially because at the time I could do a pretty decent imitation of the great actor. And so, we tested out the monitor and I delivered it, in front of the technician and in the ear of the rest of the crew as Burt Lancaster, giving just the right touch on the line, "and the coverage will last you, if you pardon the expression, from here… to eternity," referencing one of the many classic movies with which he is associated. I helped the monitor tech rehearse it a few times and after that, other crew members asked me to imitate that final line for them again.

Well, the next day, on set and ready to film, the director asked for a run through, and Mr. Lancaster spoke his lines as they scrolled. And, not only had I nailed my imitation, but he even read the final line with the same cadence and beat that I did. The problem was that the crew laughed when he read it. He did not realize that they were recalling my perfect imitation from the day before, and he got angry. "What's so funny!" he demanded. The director stammered an apology and said that it was his fault, and the crew was laughing at his error. That placated the star, and onward we went. My last image of Burt Lancaster, from that shoot, is a melancholy one.

Later that same production day, we went to a nearby school as we were using the outdoor track as the background to another part of the commercial. For whatever reason, the motor home was parked on the track, near the parking lot where the rest of the crew had their vehicles, on the other side from where we were filming. My producer needed something out of our production truck in the parking lot, and wanted it quick, so she asked me to run. I was in decent shape, and outside on a beautiful and warm Southern California day, so I ran as fast as I could. As I rounded the track, I looked up as I passed the star's motor home. I saw him sitting in the passenger seat watching me with a longing look on his face. The man who once played athlete Jim Thorpe in a movie and was known for his physical fitness was now older and was denied a recent role due to his age. Seeing me at a speedy trot seemed to touch something deep within him.

Probably the most fun I had working with a star was when I worked on an air conditioning commercial with General Chuck

Yeager, the pilot who was the first man in history to break the sound barrier. Older now, and the author of two autobiographies, he was doing the commercial and happy to do so. He was a down to earth, friendly guy. So down to earth, that on the day before when the driver brought him to the exclusive hotel that the production booked him in, he refused and asked for something basic. So, he went by choice to a Holiday Inn.

My bosses on that commercial were people with whom I had become a production family: Judy Trotter, Teddy Stewart, and Tom Cooney. My wife, Marie, a fan of flight, asked for the first and only time if she could come with me to set. The producers and assistant director said "fine!" Marie learned how repetitive and boring filming is, but she also got to see the man who was portrayed in one of her favorite moves, The Right Stuff, in the flesh. I bought multiple copies of his two books, and he was very happy to sign them. I kept one of each, and gave the others to family as Christmas gifts. And, without ever knowing it, General Yeager gave me a gift as well, a chance to perform.

Often when you see a television commercial, the spokesperson speaks to the camera about the product, as Yeager did. At the end there is usually what's called the product shot -- a closeup of it (in this case the air conditioner) with the spokesperson doing something out of the camera lens' focus, in the background. It is often too expensive to ask the lead actor, when they are a celebrity/star, to walk around in the background. I had no idea what they were going to do, but they had sized me up sometime before. Judy and Teddy, after Yeager left for the day, asked me to put on his wardrobe and to be "him" in the background.

The actor in me instinctively did what came naturally. Back even when I was doing college stage work, I realized that part of developing a character was finding how the character walked and moved. So, as I had done with Burt Lancaster in voice, I did for General Chuck Yeager in movement; I imitated him. Yeager had a short yet definitive gait and listed ever so slightly to one side. His arm movements were few and slight. So, on the same set he was filmed, they filmed the product with me in the background (from below the neck). I was pleased with my efforts when I heard that after viewing the "dailies" the next morning after the film was developed, the advertising agency for the air conditioner asked the director, "How did you get General Yeager to remain for the product shot!"

In the five years I spent working, mostly as a production assistant, on television commercials, I also had some amazing experiences on music videos.

(Let's Maybe Not) Express Yourself

My first music video was a huge production. One day, I had an old contact call me in to work on the video for Madonna's *Express Yourself* (1989). This music video was a massive undertaking that was staged over three connecting sound stages in Culver City. I was in a non-union position on a non-union shoot, and I cannot recall another time where I worked harder in my life than over the two weeks I held in that position. A highlight of this opportunity was working alongside the then young and upcoming director, David Fincher. The retro art deco sets were truly magnificent since in these early years of music videos, the record companies financed the productions. Later in the industry, the funding was put on the artist, and that's why they've changed over time. However, this Madonna one was certainly well funded.

Just as memorable, but maybe not exactly in the best way, was the star of the video. With any production, there's an intricate balance of talent, crew, and producers which can often be seen and treated in hierarchical order. The artist, in the case of music videos, is who sets the tone for a set and an experience. For this project, sadly, Madonna seemed disconnected and uncaring towards us as a crew, which I discovered slowly through observation and remaining as useful as possible on the set, but often happily invisible.

I was trained early on in my PA days to always look busy. Because smoking cigarettes on set was normal and accepted in those days, there were always the cast-off cigarette butts to be swept. With push broom in hand, I worked my way around, behind and throughout the stage as a way of keeping busy. I think it has been said that staff members using brooms often became unseen, almost invisible, and that is what happened there. My first day on the busy set, Madonna was being filmed in a manner that required the top of her chest to be exposed. To help with the effect, she wore a terry cloth robe, and kept demanding in a whining and scratchy voice, "I need more make-up on my tits!" I was about ten feet away, but her shout got the attention of all the crew, and we all got a very full visual when she dropped her robe down to her waist, exposing her full upper torso. Her act would only be more fitting if the song we were filming was titled "Expose" instead of "Express" Yourself!" Still, for me, I know that much can happen on a set. Emotions are high, and money is at stake, so I try to give grace in those moments, and I just kept on sweeping, pretending not to notice, and I moved on with the day.

Because of the non-union aspect of the shoot, the call times for crew arrival and the long hours were brutal, especially for a production assistant who was often the first on set and last to leave. On a particular night, we had all been working close to twenty hours, and Mr. Fincher ordered us to buy pizzas for everyone. After the food arrived, we were able to take what was possibly the best break in a workday I've ever experienced. It was at this moment our star came onset only to discover that all work had ceased. She stormed over to where Mr. Fincher was sitting, working on his plans for the next scene. I was nearby, sweeping and unseen. Reaching the director in his high chair, she screeched, "David, why is the crew not working?" After he replied that they were on a break, her response again began with an inquiry. "I thought this was a non-union crew," she challenged him. "It is," he meekly replied. She demanded an answer to his decision by her volcanic retort, "Then why are you letting them eat?!?!" He noticed me nearby and leaned in quietly to her and firmly said something that I believe quite satisfied her as an explanation.

Occasionally, under incredibly lucky circumstances, a production assistant gets to be a part of the action; and so it was for me on *Express Yourself*. In one segment, Madonna danced at the top of a staircase that was not all that wide. With the inclusion of the camera and crew, there was even less maneuverable space. I was told to stand off to the side, below from where she was, in order to catch her if she fell. I never needed to fulfill that role as there wasn't a misstep, and while she was kind to the dancers, I was not included in that list. At one point, they moved the camera away to prepare to set the unit for another angle and I was standing at the bottom of the steps as she maneuvered down. I held out my arm in case she wanted an assurance of stability, but she ignored it and me as she sauntered by. (I heard that on her next video she did apparently have a wild affair with the production assistant, and I am not sure what made her even notice him, based on my experience, but that's neither here nor there).

There was this one shot in the music video where the male protagonist gets into an elevator and the doors are closing. The elevator was a set piece made of wood and it was positioned within one of the massive stages. My friend and fellow PA, William, and I were tasked with closing the makeshift prop elevator doors, each of us standing on either side of the set and out of the camera range, where we, upon hearing the word "action," were to slide the doors together. The director worked with William and me so that we got the feel of the doors, so that we could slide our respective sides to join in the exact center with a firm clasp. When he began filming, we messed up a couple of the takes either by not meeting in the middle or out of sync in speed. It was a tough production, and probably because the director couldn't take his anger on the difficult star, it was redirected to us. To say he lost it does not do the moment justice. His diatribe was filled with all the words one could imagine and probably a few more. Luckily our director of photography, who was in a bit of a better headspace, came to our defense and said, "David, they are PAs, they are doing their best." We practiced another time or two and finally got the take right.

While some moments were hard, there were many good ones too. It was while working on *Express Yourself* that I got to meet a true Hollywood star. The evening was getting late, and I had been out on an errand. After parking and walking back towards the stage, another individual emerged from their car as well. He was too far away, and in the evening shadows, I couldn't see anything, but I heard his question. "Excuse me, is this the stage where Madonna is filming?" He began approaching me, and because we had explicit instructions not to allow any non-crew member on set, I only answered with, "Well, that depends on who you are…" I did not get the last word out of my mouth, because as he got closer, I realized who was now mere feet from me. "Oh, Mr. Beatty, it's you. Of course, she is right in there."

Actor and director Warren Beatty and Madonna were at what turned out to be the end of their romance while working on the film *Dick Tracy* (1990), which was still under production. I can see why their coupledom didn't last long after the project, mostly because every interaction I had with him was nicer than the first. As we walked together, he initiated constant conversation with me, asking how production was coming along. He couldn't believe my call and turnaround times, and like my dad did with his crew members, Mr. Beatty treated me like a person. It was a welcome change from what I was experiencing that week, and just those small incidents of respect and genuine quality time can make someone's day become good once again. I thank Mr. Beatty for giving me back the little things in that season of my life.

That was near the end of the production's time at the Culver City Studios lot because there were still a couple of days we needed to film at a power plant in Long Beach, California. As I left Culver Studios on our final day there, at about 3:00 a.m., I asked our assistant coordinator, Chris, what my call time was for the next morning. He was as beat up by the whole shoot as the rest of us, and barked, "It's not my job to give you a call time." In actuality though, it was, especially because the production coordinator to whom I reported had gone home earlier to catch up on sleep. These sniping matches and overall general stress that hung in the air without a break was what encompassed the making of this music video. That last exchange, though, led to me volunteering to be the first production assistant let go when they began reducing staff as the production ended.

Since no one gave me a time to report on set, I went by the last call time I had been given, which only allowed me to sleep at home for two hours before getting up, getting the truck, and heading to our new location. It was after arriving onto the power company property that I learned we weren't required to arrive until much later in the morning. I took a nap on the sunshine-warmed sidewalk, basking in the heat and with the assurance that like all productions, this one too would conclude. Despite what this experience left me with, I moved onto another set, with is a much better story to tell because I got to work alongside one of my favorite classic rock bands of all time.

When I Became the Lead Singer of Aerosmith for Five Minutes

On one rare day off between production jobs, I purchased a new compact disc, just released by the rock band Aerosmith, called *Pump* (1989). The song *Love in an Elevator* was already receiving radio and video airplay and the rest of the album was just as rocking. While listening to it, I received a call from the production coordinator from *Express Yourself* asking me if I could work as a production assistant on their next video. For. Aerosmith. I was set to receive my usual salary, but had I known what was going to happen, I would have done it for free. It was the making of the video for their next single from the band's record, a song called *Janie's Got a Gun*, which was to be directed, once more, by Mr. David Fincher. For the first day of shooting, we would be filming in a small warehouse in downtown Los Angeles. When I took the job, I thought to myself, "it cannot get better than this." Oh, but how it did.

That 24-hour workday was the only one where we filmed the band on what looked like a concert performance on a stage. Other days were reserved for filming the story part of the music video. My start wasn't on set, but I was directed to meet another production assistant at a car rental place in West Hollywood or Beverly Hills, where two town cars were waiting for us to drive. Our first stop was a nearby ritzy hotel, where we picked up the members of Aerosmith and drove them to the downtown location. I remember thinking, "This is my life. I get to drive around some of the members of Aerosmith!? It cannot get any better than this!"

This hotel specifically catered to celebrities, and as the other PA and I waited out front, I remember seeing actor Mike Myers waiting for a pick-up. More impressive was the extremely confident-looking performer, Liza Minelli, waiting in an almost royal pose with one leg bent slightly in front of the other. The offspring of famous parents, director Vincent Minelli and actress/singer Judy Garland, her gaze was only averted when the band walked out of the hotel. My fellow PA and I introduced ourselves to them, and in what I understand is representative of the dynamic of the band, the lead singer, Steven Tyler, drove alone with the other production assistant while the four musician members, including one of my favorite guitarists Joe Perry, got into my car. There I was driving on a busy freeway at 7:00 a.m. with Joe Perry sitting next to me. "It cannot get better this this," I quietly mused to myself.

On our way to the downtown location, I kept my eyes on the road and my focus on my responsibility while also trying to be a proverbial fly on the wall during their conversations in the vehicle. I remember when Joe looked over from his front seat to where the other three were sitting in the back, and politely, but firmly, asked drummer Joey Kramer to, "knock it off." Joey had brought along a handheld bean bag-type instrument that for a significant portion of our long drive, kept shaking in rhythm. He acquiesced to Perry's request.

I was relieved that the demeanor of the group was much calmer this time around, as opposed to when they made my favorite album of theirs, *Draw the Line* (1977). By this time, they had all come from a group stint in rehab and were clean and sober. They appeared at peace with one another and respectful of each other's needs, which was refreshing to see. Not going to lie, some of their conversations during our travels were almost dull. Part of me hoped for the drama. However, it was nice to hear Joe Perry share how he spent the previous day with his wife visiting Disneyland. I was also able to listen in on a little bit of rock and roll dish; a few reading the newspaper article on their once opening act, Cheap Trick, and learning they've garnered a number one hit with their new single, *The Flame* (1988). Joe Perry sounded off on his opinion of Cheap Trick's lead guitarist, Rick Nielsen. Perry felt it was silly for Neilson to remain dressed in the thin, goofy baseball cap that he wore, and that perhaps it was time for him to mature in his persona. As of writing this, just like Aerosmith, Cheap Trick is still rocking, and Rick Nielsen is still dressing in his unique way. You have to respect his not changing in this business after all these years. As we arrived at the shoot, the band asked me to help them carry their guitar cases into the building. The five of us walked in, me carrying Aerosmith's instruments, and I thought, once again, "it cannot get any better than this!"

Once inside, I checked with my coordinator as the band shuffled backstage to change into concert wardrobe, hair, and make-up. Lead singer Steven Tyler, having arrived with the other vehicle and driver, entered a few minutes later as well. During the shoot I had a chance to share a few brief words with him and was happily surprised at how down-to-earth he was. His image of the rock 'n roll "bad guy," was diminished further when I encountered him later that day exploring a dark corner of the abandoned warehouse admiring the graffiti and art that covered the walls. He called me over and began speaking as a modern-day archeologist. "Look at these," he said pointing to the paintings on the concrete, "they look like pentagrams, like someone was doing devil worship or something."

While these interactions had been magnificent, the best memory was yet to come. After I deposited their instruments in their dressing room, I was put to task making "cue cards" for Mr. Tyler. Because he was lip-syncing to a pre-recorded track, his wording needed to be exact. Even though I had the lyrics in front of me, I knew them by heart having listened to the album every day since its release. If anything, this task further cemented the words into my mind, and became part of the fun to come.

After completing the cue cards, I went to my usual busy activity—sweeping. Then I heard a discussion between the crew. "We need someone to stand in for lighting purposes," said the technician. When filming, they often place a person where the lead actor will stand so that they can test how the lighting shines against the skin. The director looked around set and pointed me out to the assistant director and said, "get *him*." And so there I was. Standing behind the lead singer's microphone. All around me were the guitar stands with band assistants putting gear into place and assembling the drummer's kit. And while I am standing in the middle of Aerosmith's stage, behind Tyler's mic stand, already draped with his signature scarves, I thought yet again, "it cannot get better than this!"

While I remained in place for lighting purposes, one by one, having gotten into wardrobe, the members of the band took to our stage, grabbed their instruments, and stood in their designated spots. At one point I looked to my left, my right, and behind me and was overwhelmed with the notion that I was standing on stage with members of one of my favorite bands, with me getting to play the part of Steven Tyler. No doubt by now you know the thought that was going through my mind at this moment, and yet, it did get even better than that.

Mind you, I have been on sets. I met Batman and gazed down a fake elevator shaft to where the Bat-Cave was supposed to be. I sat amidst a witch's convention on the set of *Bewitched* where I also played word games with the stars. I was teased by Elizabeth Montgomery. I watched Sally Field at work in *The Flying Nun*. And I stood on the bridge set of *Star Trek's* Enterprise ship. It was this day, however, in this dingy old building in downtown Los Angeles on a music video shoot, when another life-altering moment would shatter anything I had previously experienced.

As the band gathered on stage with their wardrobe on and their hair and make-up in place, there was still one person missing. Frustrated at the wait, Fincher asked his assistant how much longer Tyler's preparation would take. After some back on forth on the radio, the assistant reported it would be another 10-15 minutes. The director briefly spoke to the crew about what he was going to do, and then gave instructions to the band members. "We are going to do a full run through of the song. Guys," he said indicating the actual musicians on the platform, "do what you normally do on stage, and you," he said looking at me, "stay behind the mic and don't move."

Wait, what? Stay behind the mic and don't move? It clicked into place and suddenly a dream I didn't even know I had was coming true. Not too many years before was I alone in my bedroom performing this very same scenario, pretending to be Steven Tyler and singing every single song. Now, for about four or five minutes, I actually was. The beginning riff of the song began, and immediately chills covered me completely. It's one that still goes through me today when I hear those chords, knowing every lyric and traveling back to when I did not move a muscle, but mouthed the words while Tyler's vocals came forth from the speakers. And the band played their silent instruments right alongside me. During a guitar solo, Joe Perry leaned against me as he pretended to play the piece, and my life felt complete. Yes, for a little over five minutes, I was the lead singer of Aerosmith. It was something I will never forget, and I was on cloud nine all the rest of that day's shoot, until I was unfortunately brought back down by Mr. Perry.

In the days before GPS, I had to rely on a map that had been researched and printed out for me (shocking). Because we all worked on the production as a non-union crew, we were about 24 hours from when we began in the a.m. and were now headed back to their hotel. Perry, back to sitting shotgun in the driver's seat, kept suggesting that I get off at different streets. I explained to him I was unfamiliar with downtown Los Angeles, and that I was more comfortable sticking to the map and directions I had in front of me, just to be safe. Even though we left well before Steven Tyler, my car arrived later at the hotel. His vehicle turned a corner and drove in front of ours as we entered the hotel property. Agitated, and demonstrating a little tension that perhaps existed between band members, Perry was upset and started yelling at me. "We left before Steven, and now he's arriving *ahead* of us!"

I apologized for any inconvenience and assured him and the others that I was just following the directions I had been given. In frustration and putting a dismissive end to the moment, Perry said, "What the f--- does it matter?!" While it seemed to matter much to him, I kept my mouth shut and left my production booklet with an Aerosmith logo on the front of it in the vehicle. I was going to ask for signatures but decided not to press my luck. While that moment was a bit of an unfortunate way to end the highlight of my life, at that point I couldn't be brought down. While Madonna caused me doubts in production, Aerosmith gave me hope. And I wouldn't have changed a thing.

The filming lasted a few more days after we shot the band's part. The story in the film, a lecherous dad (played by actor Christopher Guest) preyed upon his daughter who exacted her revenge by shooting him–had yet to be filmed. I drove the actress around in a RV that had been rented to double as her dressing room and we shot in a dark neighborhood street near Hollywood. We later settled in for a couple days of filming at the beautiful Greystone Mansion, a property now owned by the City of Beverly Hills, and used by many productions, with some additional night shooting in Griffith Park.

This time around, I was tasked with the usual duties of a production assistant. Perhaps my favorite moment was the brief period I was asked to follow actress Lesley Ann Warren with an umbrella to protect her from the sun's rays. This lovely, talented performer was delightful to walk with, and I was happy to spend the day with her.

Eventually, she recognized the silliness of it all, and decided she would hold her own umbrella, so it was time for me to turn to a new task. No doubt I found a broom to keep me looking busy.

At Griffith Park, we shot in the evening a scene where police converge on the sight of the discovered deceased father's body. In the maverick music video fashion of the day, I was thrust into a role. As PAs, we needed to direct the actors who were arriving on set where to park their cars. Vehicle after vehicle would roll up, the driver's window down, and the person inside would say, "I am here to play the cop." We soon began to answer, "Yeah, you and about forty other guys!"

As the crime scene shot commenced, Fincher decided at the last minute he wanted a pretend news crew to be among the police. PAs were pressed into service. I was wearing a blue and white rugby shirt which made me easy to spot. Only in the long version of the video, one that I cannot find online no matter how hard I try, was my long-distance part viewable. As the shot rose above the body of the father, and uniformed police converged, you can see two figures as well, one holding a video camera, carried by my fellow PA William, and me with a microphone in hand, approaching the scene.

The camera wasn't close enough to catch our faces, but each time we filmed the shot, I thrust out the microphone and asked a different question, taking delight in breaking up the seriousness of the others, knowing that their faces would not be on camera. "Is it true that this is the latest Elvis sighting?" The actors laughed, and then became playfully annoyed that my question made them break character. But I did it again and again with a different joke. These days are long, and you have to throw fun in there every once in a while. I loved making people laugh, and doing so when they were not supposed to add some extra hilarity to an already dream experience. Growing up on film sets made them a comfortable realm for me.

Some years after this shoot, there was another video released for the song *Young Lust*. It was created using behind-the-scenes footage from recent adventures of the band, and sure enough, at around minute 3:47 in the video, there is a one-second shot with a couple of band members on one side of the stage and me on the other in the lead spot. My face appears in shadow, maybe because when they put this video together, I had not signed a release form, but if you can keep from blinking at minute 3:47, you can see me!

Though I worked mostly on television commercials during my production assistant days, I enjoyed a few more opportunities to work with my favorite artists and bands on music videos. I spent a day with the Moody Blues as we made the video for their song *Say It With Love* (1992), but alas, the video we shot was scrapped and replaced with another. Though I put Aerosmith up there as one of my favorite video experiences, there were two others that were significant. The first, due to the kindness of the artist, and the second as it connected me to my mother through a celebration of MGM Musicals.

The Nicest Man in the World was Named Peter Frampton

By far, the famous star who I worked with, whom I respected even more after working alongside, was Peter Frampton. As I've stated, my dad's television shows were examples where kindness spread throughout the crew, and it made for a more relaxed set than ones where stars or producers were strict and unpersonal. Peter Frampton would have fit in extremely well on a Harry Ackerman Production. I worked with Frampton on a video for his song *More Ways Than One* (1989), and I reported to the Sunset Gower Studios where we filmed the piece. I was the only production assistant hired for this relatively small shoot, and that kept me busy in good ways. Most of the crew was flown in from London, and like other non-union shoots, it took about 24 hours to do our filming. It was always a special joy for me whenever I worked at this studio, because it is the same one where my mother did *Father Knows Best*, and later *Get A Life*. The little connections I could always keep to my parents and their contributions thrilled me every time. After Frampton arrived, he wanted to tune his guitars and adjust his instruments' straps. I was sent over to help. What a privilege. We stood and made small talk while he had me drape one of his guitars over my shoulders as he adjusted what was needed. He then began tuning the strings, and to be so close to the man still known for the album *Frampton Comes Alive* (1976) was a thrill in itself, but only kept getting better.

Though I didn't make it on camera this time around, I had an off-camera presence in one shot. Frampton would begin singing to the track wearing sunglasses that would eventually need to be quickly torn off his face, but because he had to play guitar during the scene, they needed someone off to the side for him to hand the glasses to. That role fell to me. When I go back and watch the video to this day, I take great delight in knowing that's me just off-screen.

It was a busy shoot as we only had a day to accomplish everything. When the filming finally concluded, the crew began to pack up all of the equipment and by that time of the morning, the record company execs had gathered on stage and were congratulating everyone on a job well done, assuring Frampton that this song was going to be a hit. To celebrate, one of the executives brought out a bottle of champagne along with some paper cups. The production department heads were called together into a circle along with Frampton, the record company representatives, and the director. Champagne was poured and someone began a toast. Across the stage, and out of the way of their celebration, I was doing my part in getting the stage back in order by, as you can no doubt guess, sweeping the floor. Just beyond the first few words of the toast, I heard Frampton yell, "Wait!" He walked over to where I was, took me by the arm, and said, "Come here." I followed him into the circle where he took a cup, poured a splash of champagne into it, handed it to me, and then retrieved his cup that was held by someone else. Once I had champagne in hand, he looked at the execs and lead crew members and said, "Now, we can toast." So, we did. My father was someone who saw value in every member of the production crew. Peter Frampton brought that spirit and courtesy back in a way that reminded me of what Ackerman Productions represented. I was so honored by the gesture, and doubly proud that we share the same birthday (though different birth years). Whenever I'm asked who the nicest star is I ever worked with, top of that list is always the one and only Peter Frampton. After this shoot, I got the opportunity, through a music video, to experience some of the greats from classic movies.

Stepping Into my Mother's World Thanks to Janet Jackson

Certainly, I have worked with a lot of stars. Probably, for me, the largest gathering of them on a related job, outside of the *Bewitched* set, was due to my working on a music video that hearkened back to the days my mother worked on musicals at the famed MGM Studios. I loved those musicals as well, after my mother once took me to see *That's Entertainment* (1974) when it opened in theaters. The documentary presented the colorful and musical history of MGM Musicals, and my love for that specific film genre began that day. It was then with great delight that I was hired to work as a production assistant on a Janet Jackson music video, filmed on the backlot of Universal Studios. The song was called *Alright* (1990), and the story in which the music video takes place hearkened back to movie musicals.

On the first day of the production, I met the big band leader and singer, Cab Calloway. By then, the elderly artist played himself in the video and was also portrayed at a younger age by another actor. Mr. Calloway was outside ready to do his shot when I was asked to go to his trailer for an errand. I noticed some gold necklace jewelry on a table by the door, and I felt that leaving these out in the open like that wasn't wise, so I took them with me when I returned to the artist. I handed him the necklace and explained why I brought them, and just he smiled at me, laughed, and said, "They are not real," as he handed them to his friend who was standing nearby. It might have been small, but I was thrilled to have spoken to this star whose song *Minnie the Moocher* (1931) is still a personal favorite.

In other news, I had a less-than-perfect interaction with star Cyd Charisse, but that was my fault. She was a dancer and actress from the classic MGM Studio days and appeared in a short part of the video. When I told her about my mother, who as a little girl acted in her movie *The Unfinished Dance*, I inadvertently insulted her. For many older actresses, age is a very sensitive subject. I was too consumed with the excitement of our connection and her invitation for me to cease fell on deaf ears as I blurted out "My mother worked with you when she was a little girl!" I realized as soon as I said it that Ms. Charisse was not thrilled to have a thirty-year-old man tell her that she worked with his parent when said parent was young.

Still, the highlight of the job for me was watching the fabulous dancing duo, The Nicholas Brothers, at work. Fayard and Harold Nicholas were African American siblings who are still appreciated today for their superb athletic dance abilities. They appeared in the video for less than half a minute when Janet Jackson's character crosses paths with them in an alleyway when she exits a door. I took the opportunity to watch them at work, engage in conversation, and later be introduced to their wives who were on the set watching. For me, not only a fan of musicals and dancing but who briefly studied dance as well, seeing these masters create a routine from scratch was a complete pleasure. I could watch and study how they created moves that not only showed their prowess but found ways through their abilities to complement one another.

What was disappointing about working on that shoot was how many people were unaware of who these classic musical artists were. Granted it was well over forty years since these artists were in their heyday, and most of the crew members were much younger than that, but it still hurts a little to think about it. Whether it was the fellow who asked me for whom Cyd Charisse was acting as a stand-in, or the grumpy technician who barked unkindly at the brothers when they asked for something, I was sad to realize how few people understood the depth of talent and fame in their midst.

This remains a fun video to watch today, and I particularly enjoyed helping to pull camera cable out of the way during a performance by the then new rap artist, Heavy D, during his break in the middle of the Janet Jackson tune. He later went into acting, but sadly passed away at way too young an age. What makes this particular project so special was that this one video included so many fabulous artists connected to my family story. It made me feel privileged for the chance to work on it and with the personalities I get to recall fondly.

Chapter 7

Honors Did Come for My Dad

After *The New Gidget* came to an end after two seasons and though my dad continued to be professional, a gentleman, and affable, he did not know that the series he executive produced was his last. Looking back, I feel that there could have been more success for him after Bewitched. If there was one conversation I could have with my father today, it would be around why refused to adapt to the changes that television brought in the 1970s, which is what ultimately put him out of work in the industry. Change is inevitable, and fighting it never goes well. In my mind, pushing against it hurts progress and what is sometimes necessary change. My brother James believes our dad's struggle to find work could have also been due to a back injury that ailed him for a time, but I think if it was, it was very minimal. Dad kept trying so hard, working with writers constantly, to produce new ideas.

While Dad was falling, "Uncle Bill," producer and director Bill Asher, was thriving. Dad continued working, successfully, even obtaining a Real Estate License. It ended up not being his forte, never making a sale, but he was still a name and bouncing through the industry. As I grew older, I cannot tell you how many times I remember my dad meeting with a network or production company and ultimately receiving a phone call with the news that instead of him, they hired some kid right out of college. On one occasion, my mother became so frustrated and told my father, "Why don't you call Bill Asher and tell him to do something! He has no trouble finding work!"

Though Dad and Bill remained friends, getting together at our house to place bets on football games for instance, was no more. There remains for me still a missing piece of why Dad couldn't get or keep a job beyond a small project or two during his later years.

This mystery stems from something I heard Bill Asher say shortly before his death, when he was overheard talking about my dad's heavy drinking. I wonder, "Is that why Dad couldn't get hired?"

Thankfully, the appreciation that I know warmed my father's heart came beginning with *The New Gidget* period. At the same time, my mother continued to star in plays and regularly auditioned for various television roles. Oftentimes, she was cast in stage productions that took her to different locations: Florida, Kansas City, and Canada where she was cast as the featured celebrity in the play. When she performed locally in one of these, I'd always attend as I could, but never made it to one of her out-of-town shows.

In a surprise move, during this time when my parents diligently worked to make financial ends meet, The Hollywood Chamber of Commerce awarded my father with a Star on the Hollywood Boulevard Walk of Fame. Then, they saddled him with the news: if he accepted, he had to pony up thousands of dollars for the eternal upkeep of the same. The money pays for the initial construction, the reveal event, and is added into a fund for the perpetual upkeep of the Star which is set into the sidewalk, adorned with the recipient's name and a symbol indicating the genre of show business where the awarded contributions were done. Of course, in my dad's case, it was television.

Frugal as he was, having been a child of the Depression, he actually considered not taking it. "Over my dead body are you not taking this honor," my mother had said, and she was right. With *The New Gidget*, Harry and his type of shows were back in favor. This was a much-needed opportunity in a career that had gone dark. It was right that he stepped forward to accept this recognition that unfortunately would no doubt flee into distant memory again. And so, he agreed to have his name on the famous sidewalk of the stars.

Dad took a few weeks to walk the map of available spaces that the Hollywood Chamber of Commerce provided him, listing where he could place his star. He searched and considered many factors until finding the one for him. The Harry Ackerman Walk of Fame

Star is located at 6667 Hollywood Boulevard. just east of Cherokee Avenue. The reason he chose that spot is because it's near the front door to the famed Hollywood eatery, Musso & Frank's Bar and Grille, a favorite restaurant of his and mine. The closest my father came to playing the "Hollywood game" was leading those he had business lunches with at Musso's, outside, walking them right by his star.

His star unveiling ceremony was lovely and very well-attended. Johnny Grant, the honorary Mayor of Hollywood, as well as some of the cast from *The New Gidget*, were on hand to share stories and speak on his professional behalf. I was there, looking very "Miami Vice" with my then-girlfriend Susie, and most likely because I was trying too hard to look like a Hollywood superstar, an artist who painted a portrait of the event left me out of it. However, Susie is very much included, awkwardly enough. Though that day earned me my nickname of "Hollywood" from my friend John Colorado who was in the crowd, my overcompensation was probably due to the fact that my mother was absent from the event, as she was working on a show that filmed in Canada. I wanted to be the strongest presence for my dad, but I might have gone a bit too far.

While Dad was receiving long-awaited honors, Mom was out of town. Her career was on an uptick that had her on the move. The program she was working on when Dad received his star was one premiering on the new Fox Network, *The New Adventures of Beans Baxter* (1987). Another premiere at the time was The *Tracey Ullman Show* (1987-1990) which featured a little-known Matt Groening cartoon segment known as *The Simpsons* (1989 -). As we all know, that soon developed into its own series. Rounding up the new series line-up on Fox included *Married with Children* (1987-2002).

The New Adventures of Beans Baxter followed the life of a young boy named Beans, played by the young and very talented actor Jonathan Ward. Elinor was cast as Beans' mother on the show. In the premise of the story, Beans was a secret spy, his identity unbeknownst to his parents, and though the synopsis might not have been of much interest, the performers were. Playing the evil nemesis was actor Kurtwood Smith, whose career seemed to skyrocket after this show aired. The supporting cast over time included others like comedian Rick Overton, who is one of the funniest people on the planet in this author's opinion. I had the opportunity to work with him once on an HBO commercial about upcoming comedy specials, and, well, tales of that encounter could be its own book. Alongside George Wallace, Rick Overton is the definition of funny. There was a specific episode where Nixon burglar G. Gordon Liddy played an operative who fell for my mother's character. Though some found him kind of scary around the set, my mother found him fascinating. When a light broke on set and a crew member went to pick it up, Liddy yelled to him not to touch it with his bare hands. He added something like, "That contains a substance we use; when mixed with the right chemicals, it can kill on contact." Fascinating indeed!

The show never took with the home audience, so it was ultimately canceled. Mom had worked so hard on that program and sacrificed a lot to do it. It was filmed in Canada, which seemed to be the classic move at that time, and the rigorous schedule took my mother away from home for a number of weeks at a time. It was the reason she couldn't be present at her husband's star unveiling. It was a hard period, but very much speaks to her work ethic.

During these later years in her career, there was an interesting development my mother began seeing now as she was playing mom characters of older children. "I had the distinction of being fired from [the same show] twice!" she recalled. *Highcliffe Manor* (1979) was a series attempt that was originally cast with her, but after the first table read, she was let go and replaced by another actress. Ten days later, she was re-cast on the show in a different role, and they continued rehearsing for the upcoming filming that would air before a live studio audience. After the network run-through and during a dress rehearsal where the same group of people observed the show to offer feedback, she was fired again. Who finally replaced her? One of the producers! Knowing the machinations about the business,

Dad had concluded that this was the producer's plan all along. But all was not finished for Elinor Donahue. A door opened for her right then, which brought her to the attention of a whole new fan base.

Coincidentally, that door opened because she was replacing an actress. *Get a Life* (1990-1992) was a show produced by Chris Elliott, who is known to many today from his role on *Schitt's Creek* (2015-2020). He has consistently proven himself to be a talented comedian, actor, and writer. Elliott was the son of one of the members of the Bob and Ray comedy team, Bob Elliott. Mom truly lucked out on her audition if I may say so myself. Told only that she was the mother of a paperboy, she was able to think back to when my little brother James had a paper route at age 12. So, at the audition, she pretended as if she were talking to a pre-teen. Little did she know that the part was for the adult-aged Chris Elliott. Still, it somehow worked, and after being cast, she continued to play that character as if she were talking to Chris Elliot, the 12-year-old boy. There are still many fans of that show today.

She was able to play opposite Elliott's real-life father, and a funny shtick throughout the series involved the parents always being dressed in their pajamas. A win-win if my mother had an early call or wanted to go to bed once she got home at the end of the day. But the second season shifted to a different direction. No matter the current success, Bob Elliott refused to do another season of his son's show. The producers were forced to change the format, and while Elinor and Bob pre-filmed some scenes for the second season, the overall change in the program bombed ratings, resulting in a cancellation of the show. There was so much appreciation for that first season of *Get a Life* for Mom. It brought her back to the Sunset Gower Studios, on the same stage where she filmed *Father Knows Best* so many years earlier! She enjoyed being on episodic television again, and it gave her passion to focus on while Dad's health began to deteriorate.

During what became the final years of his life, I got to hang out with Dad more often. With Mom away working, and since I was one of his sons who lived close, we made frequently plans for me to come over to the house, and "screen a movie" over dinner. This meant sitting in my old bedroom, now converted into an entertainment center, and watching a rented VHS video tape on the large screen television in his entertainment center "office." Usually over his guilty favorite, Stouffer's Cream Chipped Beef over toast, we would consume our food, and sip at wine or beer and watch a movie. Before or after, our conversations went to some aspect of show business.

There is one occurrence I remember, because it led to one of the three times I saw my stoic dad cry, and by cry, I mean, get tears in his eyes while his voice choked back the ebbing tears. The first was a couple of decades before at our Valley Meadow Road home. I got up one morning in 1968 and saw my older brother and my mother sobbing in each other's arms. My dad escorted me to the living room, out of the way of their grief, and we sat down on one of the smaller settees near the television. In the same place where my mother first pointed herself out to me on the television screen my dad sat strangely silent next to me. "Dad," I asked, "what's wrong with Mom and Brian?" He tried, but uncharacteristically mumbled. I realized later that he was holding his own emotions at bay, but I surely did not hear him correctly. So, I asked him "what did you say?" He repeated his words but what my young ears heard was, "The candy shop died." That made no sense, so I reflected what I heard from him, "What, the candy shop died?" Almost frustrated he turned to me and carefully, stoically said the words, the seriousness of the moment reflected in his very wet eyes, "Kennedy was shot… and died." Though I was an infant when President Kennedy was killed, his brother Robert, who was running for president, was also killed. For my parents who I later learned were Kennedy Democrats, this news was especially tragic. Tears from my dad were infrequent, but the next two times I saw them, they were as part of our at-home movie nights.

He was very upset and told me about a letter he received. He was not only upset at the well-written fiery prose contained in the letter, but also because of his part in causing the anger. My dad helped the producer of a tv movie biography of Lucille Ball by giving background of his experiences on *I Love Lucy*. However, in addition to what he shared on the record, there was a piece that was never meant to be mentioned to others.

As I have grown older, I sometimes meet people who interviewed my dad, for a book, or on a topic, and sometimes he would share an opinion or observation with the writer, always carefully presented. He would literally say "this is off the record," or "what I am about to say is not to be shared." Unfortunately, my dad lunched with a producer who wanted Lucille Ball's daughter, Lucie Arnaz, to put her stamp of approval on the project, which she did not want to do. It appears that in order to coerce Lucie to be a part of the project, the producer shared with her something my dad said that was not for any other ears, especially hers. My dad felt that the producer shared the comments with Lucie Arnaz to suggest that "if you do not join my project, this is the story that will be told."

And so it was that Lucie Arnaz heard a story or two that my dad told the producer, off the record, regarding activity that her dad, Desi Arnaz, and mine engaged in with women who were not their wives. My dad may have been divorced from his first wife at the time, but Desi was not. Dad received a letter from Luci Arnaz's husband, actor Larry Luckinbull, and it was explosive. All I remember from reading it was the first lines, "You are no friend of Desi's, as no friend of Desi's would ever…" I looked up from reading it and saw the sorrow in my dad's eyes and the response letter he was to mail the next day, giving a better accounting of the circumstances around his sharing the story. On another movie night, I was relieved when my dad, smiling the smile of the forgiven, presented me with Mr. Luckinbull's response, which graciously accepted my dad's apology and explanation. To this day, though, my dad's contributions appear excised from the Arnaz projects about I Love Lucy, and I have to admit, that my dad is responsible for burning that bridge.

The final tears were ones of joy. I chose a movie he had not seen for that evening. By the end of Kevin Costner's starring role in *Field of Dreams*, I looked at my dad, and there were the tears pooling in his eyes. In a film about redemption for the protagonist and contributions by people long passed, his only comment was, "Wow, everyone needs to see this movie." One of my brothers came over afterwards, and I remember my dad thrusting the video in his hand and all but demanding, watch this. Thankfully, appreciation for Dad's past contributions, as honor-filled as his star on the Hollywood Walk of Fame, was soon to come his way.

Dad's last honor was bestowed upon him shortly before he died, and as luck would have it, I was with him, and able to assist in what came as a surprising challenge. A heavy smoker until his 30's, he contracted and was treated for throat cancer. It affected his vocal cords, which became scratchy sounding when he spoke, no longer affording him the sonorous tones he once enjoyed. He was active in a group known as The Caucus of Writers Producers and Directors. Every year they had a ceremony where a member was honored, and around 1990 it was Dad who was chosen for the honor.

For some reason, my mother could not go, perhaps her work on *Get a Life* is what prompted her to suggest that I be my dad's plus one at the ceremony. So, there we two Ackerman men were, in our tuxedoes at Chasen's restaurant for the festivities. There was lots of activity and conversation in the room and at our table. The downside is that this was back in the day when smoking cigarettes in restaurants was the norm, and there were a lot of smokers present. The cloud hung like a scented veil throughout the room. Except for knowing I would need to dry clean my tux after the event, the atmosphere did not bother me, however it adversely affected my dad's healed, yet damaged throat. Halfway through the meal, he lost his voice. He leaned over and croaked in my ear, that I would have to make his speech, as he could not talk any longer above his scratchy whisper.

As a show biz kid who loved the stage, I had no problem with it. My dad, though, left nothing to chance. He pulled out one of his buck slips from his coat pocket, and his blue felt tipped pen and quickly and carefully wrote my dialogue. When the presentation came, I stood up in front of the gathered industry members, stifled a laugh, and read the following words (he made sure that I would not forget to introduce myself!) *I'm Peter Ackerman. My father has laryngitis. He has asked me to say to you – This is a banner year for me – my doctors have pronounced me cured of an illness that often proves to be fatal. Now – this honor. To be chosen by you peerless people – the best in the industry – is an honor I will never forget. It is a highlight of my life – and I thank you for giving it to me.*

His words were delivered through me, and they received a thunderous applause. To this day, I feel so honored that I got to experience this appreciation for my father by his show business contemporaries. The opportunity for him to reflect on his life's work and know that it was appreciated meant the world to us all. Additionally, I began to see, and deeply appreciate not only my own parents but also the extended family of those with whom they worked, especially as I got to know them through the years.

The Fictional Family

As the reader may know, "family" often goes beyond the idea of blood relatives. I first noticed our extended "fictional" family through my mom. The people I saw her with on the screen would sometimes reach out and phone her at home. This melding of the television world and our real life at home distilled in me the realization that people who regularly act together can develop into a family beyond the life of the series on which they appeared.

During the days of *Father Knows Best,* Betty Anderson's relationship with her siblings echoed that of Elinor's with Billy Gray and Lauren Chapin. Elinor recalls the strong bond between those two young ones that caused them to sometimes team up on her, just as younger siblings did. It was one of those relational elements that the cast members discussed and reminisced on during a few reunion shows in the 1970s. They eventually made two specials: *The Father*

Knows Best Reunion, and *Father Knows Best: Home for Christmas*, both from 1977. Elinor remains friends with her former cast members, and her TV mom, Jane Wyatt, remained a mother -figure companion throughout her life.

Jane Wyatt was an accomplished actress, and like my mother, also had a connection to *Star Trek,* playing Spock's mother, Amanda, in the series and in one of the films. She was Elinor's "other mother" and though I wasn't able to meet Jane until I was in my mid-twenties, I sensed growing up how energized my mother would be following their visits. Before meeting her, my only interaction with the *Father Knows Best* cast would be when Billy Gray occasionally called our home.

I finally met Jane Wyatt in person when she attended my aforementioned wedding in 1987, and she was in a celebratory mood. She'd had a few drinks, and at a festive wedding with old friends and new ones, why not? Later in the evening, she all but attached herself to Marie, my wife of only a few hours, and me, joyously saying, "I love Episcopal wedding services. They are beautiful, to the point, and *short*!" She stated repeatedly that evening that she was my other "grandmother," and I watched as my Nana looked on with a little steam and scowl. After a beat, Nana proclaimed proudly, "I am your *only* grandmother!" While that is true, Jane will always be a part of my fictional family.

After an Emmy Awards show, my mother shared a story about Jane that became a favorite of mine. When the cast from *Father Knows Best* gathered together to make an announcement at an Emmy Awards Ceremony, they were in the Green Room waiting area before heading on stage. Really, this cast was so much like their characters, I want to stress that. When the stage hand came in and said, "You are on in five, please follow me to the wings (of the stage)," Jane opened up her handbag and said in that upper-class accent, "Well, I guess the sun is over the yardarm!!!" and took a healthy swig of her evening cocktail from a tiny airline bottle of vodka. She offered the same to the others, who all declined, as they all walked to present.

For some reason, I find this moment elegant and endearing; a kind lady taking the edge off before heading on stage, so matter-of-factly. I am glad I got to know her and am forever grateful that during her lifetime she was a real companion and parental figure to my own mother.

Many of the actors from the shows both my parents were attached to became extended family. I mean, I got to grow up with an "aunt" who was attractive, blue-eyed, and blonde with a pixie sense of humor, who did wiggle her nose for me once. I carry fond memories of hanging out in an acting class with one of the "Gidgets," and going to school with a fellow who played my mother's son on a series.

I was finally able to meet Billy Gray and Lauren Chapin during autograph shows in the 1990s. As a showbiz fan, I used to go to these celebrity signings often, and always attended the one held a couple of times a year at the Beverly Garland Holiday Inn in Studio City. I think after my first show I convinced my mother to do one and acted as her intermediary, which granted me free access to every show I attended afterwards. Yes, such an awesome perk! My first one is where I met Billy. It was an instant familial rapport. I felt like I knew Billy; knew him like an uncle. It reached a point where I would pass messages between him and my mother, usually "Hello," or "Tell your mom I received the nice note that she sent me." He's a very cool guy, and it is always a delight when I run into him.

Lauren Chapin was the final cast member I met, and it was also at a collector's show, but meeting her will always stand out more vividly in my memory. She was there as part of a two-day event. I met her on the second day when my mother was not present. I should add that newly married and a new dad, I was going through a time in my life where we husbands/fathers gain a bit of weight, *cough, cough*. Though I was trying to get back to my normal range, people in my family had noticed the gain and I was self-conscious about it. After meeting Lauren and her daughter at the show, she mentioned to me as we were parting, "You know, you are very handsome, and

I disagree with your mom, I don't think you are too heavy at all!" I know she thought she was speaking in kindness, but to me, that was the most backhanded compliment ever spoken indeed. It felt like a knife to the self-confidence, but I remember it now with laughter and the knowledge that she spoke with good intentions, as her sweet nature always did.

Billy Gray is still an occasional presence in our lives. My youngest brother, Christopher, who amongst other things announces motorcycle races in Southern California, has run into "Uncle Billy" on occasion when he, as a motorcycle enthusiast, has shown up to watch the sport. Like Chris, I am certainly grateful to have this extended family as a part of my life as they are an important part of our mom's.

Of course, with family connections, there is always the impact when a death occurs. I was about to get my first lesson in that life course, when my dad's health took an unexpected, dramatic turn for the worse.

Death's Cameo Appearance

Death is one of those never-wanted guests whom we know can show up at any time but assume won't. But that's not true. Following New Year's Day in 1991, since my dad having some trouble breathing, my mother took him to St. Joseph's hospital in Burbank, CA. A heavy smoker until he quit in his 30s and a daily drinker throughout his life, Dad was beginning to experience several health challenges. He had suffered lower back and knee problems for as long as I could remember and had been hospitalized briefly about ten years before during back surgery. Then in the late '80s, he was diagnosed with throat cancer. My father had a sonorous vocal tone, which I inherited. The kind of voice where people would say to us, "You should read the news," or "Have you ever thought about doing radio?" Following radiation, however, his tone turned understandably raspy.

I am grateful that when death decided to come for my dad, it came at a time when his popularity had soared again. He was the

Executive Producer of *The New Gidget,* had been awarded a star on the Hollywood Walk of Fame, saw all of his children get married, and was able to be there at the birth of his first grandchildren. Most importantly, he ended his days with his wife Elinor, who he lived a full and passionate life alongside.

Perhaps fittingly, for a man who is so indelibly connected to Classic Television, the event following his funeral played out as the kind of situation you'd see on one of his television comedies. It remains my favorite memory from an otherwise very painful day. An after-funeral reception was held at the lovely home of Uncle Bill Asher and his then-wife, actress Joyce Bulifant. Joyce's son, John Asher, was serving up cocktails and I remember seeing faces of people whom I had not seen together since I was a child. As people were piling their plates with food, I suddenly heard the panicked voice of a woman. "Harry? Where's Harry? Harry!" We all froze and looked to the source of the cry. Joyce continued to call out for Harry. We all began looking to one another, as if asking, "Who is going to remind her we buried him an hour ago?" Finally, she caught herself and explained to us that Harry was also the name of their dog, who had gotten out of the house! Hearty, relieved laughter permeated the moment, and it was just what was needed.

Should there be any doubt that I inherited the show business genes from my parents, the week after my father's death would provide sufficient evidence. I kept my commitment to perform a role on *Days of Our Lives* that week, which I had been cast in just a couple of days before Dad passed. Additionally, on the Friday evening before the funeral, we were supposed to go to a viewing of an unauthorized television biography on Lucille Ball and Desi Arnaz, for which my dad was interviewed by the producers. Sadly, Dad never got to see *Lucy and Desi: Before the Laughter* (1991). He had been excited by the prospect of the project and the fact that he was written into the script and portrayed by an actor. Instead of attending the screening, the producers were nice enough to send us a recording that we enjoyed watching at home, in tribute to him, on the evening before his funeral. The actor cast as Harry Ackerman looked enough like my dad but was written in no way like him. It brought some laughs. It brought some levity to a week that really needed it.

Saturday came and we arrived at Forest Lawn, Burbank for the funeral. One of the first people to approach us was Uncle Bill, who regrettably informed us that, "Liz is not coming." Funerals bring out a lot, and they can serve as miniature reunions for the different phases of our lives. I think my mother hoped that this woman, once a good friend, would attend the funeral to at least to pay her respects to Harry. But she never showed. Perhaps she stayed away because she felt it wasn't the right gesture after not having been a part of our lives for so many years. Sally Field hadn't shown either, though Dad had a heavy hand in her early career. That didn't surprise me, however, as I remembered him having called over to Ms. Field's office to ask her to lunch while they were both working on the Warner Bros. lot a few years back. Whether she returned the call or not, the lunch never happened.

Not focusing entirely on the no-shows, the funeral was attended by so many, including members from *Get a Life*. Mom had continued to work on set, taking lunch and after-work breaks to head to the hospital to visit Dad. She is a professional, through and through. What's left when two become one? The re-shuffling of the family dynamic suddenly occurs when these events happen in life, with everyone defining new roles or old routines.

Mom's New Marriage

Elvis Presley appeared on the far fringes of my life in a couple of ways, though I never met him. My mother was an early casting choice for one of his movies. Though she can't recall which one, it's likely it was produced after she and my dad were married.

Though excited to hear from her agent that she was going to be in the film, she soon got word that she was out of the production. The explanation we were given was that Elvis preferred his leading ladies to be unmarried; oh boy, what a reason! But no matter, there would be another failed chance to meet the entertainer yet to occur.

My younger brothers Chris and James attended The John Thomas Dye Day School in Bel Air California for a few years. One of Chris' classmates happened to be Elvis' daughter, Lisa Marie Presley. He was excited when he heard from her that her dad was coming to see her the night of their school holiday performance. Alas, whether it was a spoken hope or a change of plans, he never showed up that evening. Yet still, Elvis is one degree separated from my mother in a significant way. The man who became my stepfather in 1992 worked with The King.

Louis Genevrino and my mother first met when they were paired for her dancing routines during a show for Share Inc. He reached out later to my dad, who was always willing to help someone navigate the production end of the entertainment business. Lou wanted to speak with him in regard to a project he had in mind for another actress.

Lou was acquainted with mother and father for years. Lou worked as a dancer, both on Broadway and on television. He may have even been pointed out to me on screen, as my mother always did that for dancers with whom she worked. "Oh, look!" she would say. "There's Louis!" As a dancer herself, and one who was hired to be in a Vegas Chorus line but later had to back out because she was cast in *Father Knows Best*, she always proudly remained a member of the dance community.

Lou was hired in the mid-1960s to perform as one of the male dancers on the *Elvis 1968 Comeback Special*. He remembers at some point he walked through a saloon door and pretended to take a hit from the singer in a western dance scene. That may have ended any Elvis tie to my family, but my mother found another love of her life. Lou was one of the many people on the periphery of my parent's lives. Following my dad's death in 1991, he entered into my mother's life as a supporting friend. They attended church together, enjoyed coffee after, and a deeper attraction was eventually revealed.

It was a little over a year after my dad passed away that Mom and Lou were married in a Saturday afternoon service at a church in Studio City, California. She proudly enjoyed the moment her sons walked her down the aisle to give her away. All of her sons, that is, but one.

It had been a tough year for me. I'm not sure if my dad's death hit me harder than my brothers or if I lacked the emotional maturity to process the experience. Regardless, the period of time between my dad's death and Mom and Lou's marriage seemed non-existent. I had no desire to look at their relationship from her point of view. Narrowly, all I could see was that my dad had just died and now she was marrying someone else.

With life experience, my understanding of time has matured. For my mother, those months following my dad's death were long. Every day was filled with adjusting, mourning, and attempting to live life as a single woman. Those twelve months between her husband's death and her marriage to Lou were filled with learning and adapting. Being single and navigating dating. I could check out easily from the reality of his passing. I mourned in pockets. She lived with it every hour of every day. Her desire to settle into a new phase of her life was ever present.

When I reluctantly admitted to her that I couldn't go to her and Lou's wedding, I knew she was disappointed, but she never tried to change my mind. My grandmother spoke to me however, trying to reason with me. Though I loved her immensely, it was the one request I was too trapped in my emotional turmoil to grant. Another relative sent me a tersely written letter, telling me how my dad would be very disappointed in me. I spoke to them later, claiming how I knew my dad would have respected, not agreed with, but respected my decision. Especially as I was very open about my feelings.

Having known Lou now these many years, I'm not surprised that it was he who ultimately ended my guilt and put the discussion of my absence at their wedding day to rest. "I get it," he said to me one day. "Of course, your mother's disappointed, but Peter, you had to do what felt right to you." We spoke about grief and losing those you love, and how you have to make the best choice for your own emotional situation.

On their wedding day, the same hour they were in a church in Studio City, California, I was at Forest Lawn Cemetery, visiting my father's grave. The connection I felt to him there was palpable. All I could hear in that moment was him laughing the way he would at something obvious. He would have asked me, while I was pulling at blades of grass that surrounded his headstone, "What are you doing *here*?"

It was then, right then and there, with my dad's voice ever present, that I realized I should be at the wedding. But instinctively I knew, running to my car and driving down to that church would make it about me. So, I sat with my dad instead. I may love Hollywood, but that was way too much of a "Hollywood" move to make. I had made my choice, and I had to live with it. And the one who reminds me I can live comfortably with that choice is Lou, the man who is the grandfather to my children and has stepped into the "dad" role many times for me in my adult life. A supporter and encourager, he is wise and always ready to laugh with me, just like my dad. He is a blessing to all of us who know him.

My parents were married almost thirty years. As I'm writing this, it seems Lou and my mother have surpassed that timeline. They will do so happily, faithfully, and in support of one another in the Palm Desert area of California. Around the time they met and married, I moved from working on television commercials and music video productions into the family business of television production.

Chapter 8

My Move into Television Production Work

After my dad died, I moved out of the world of television commercial and music video production and closer into the family realm, when someone I had worked with in the past, now the assistant to an Executive Producer, invited me to interview for an office production assistant on a 1991 Warner Bros. series called *The Human Target*. Starring Rick Springfield, it was a very good program, a little bit like the spy series, *Mission Impossible*. Its only problem was that the network decided to air it on Monday evenings against Monday Night Football. It did not stand a chance!

The benefit of working on a studio lot was being able to make friends in all the departments where I could get a line on what other shows were gearing up with their office personnel. Through my contacts I found out that Frank Sinatra's daughter, Tina, was executive producing a mini-series about her father, Frank! When I went to be interviewed by her, I went with some trepidation. Years before, my father fell way of favor with Mr. Sinatra.

Apparently, they knew each other in my dad's CBS days and worked well together. They did until one day Frank held up rehearsals, which included a number of musicians, and my dad gave Frank Sinatra a talking-to about keeping people waiting! After that, he once told me, that whenever he was at an event, after Frank saw my dad in the room, he would purposely turn his back upon him. I wondered if this would stop me from getting the job on *Sinatra*, the miniseries.

I was brought into Tina's office and sat across her desk from her, after being introduced to her by her assistant. Alone in her office, my palms began to sweat, especially after she asked "Peter

Ackerman…are you one of *the* Ackermans?" Hiding my nervousness in an office space that began to feel stuffy, I admitted that I was the son of Harry Ackerman. As it turned out, that fact got me the job! Tina shared with me that when she was trying to break out on her own as an actress, my father cast her in one of his shows, and with that positive news, I was offered the job. Those six months became my favorite production job ever. At the time, paperwork took a long time to turn around. A crew member, like the head of the property department, had to sometimes outlay money for something, and because we did not have an unlimited budget, they needed their reimbursement sooner. So, because the production office was a few miles off of the Warner Bros. lot, my responsibility became the daily shuffling of the paperwork. I began at the office where I picked up all of the necessary reimbursement items submitted from the stage personnel and drove to Warner Bros. where I had the use of a bicycle. I would take my bike and drop off paperwork to the Vice President in charge of our production's office and pick up the approved paperwork that was always waiting me. Next, I bicycled over to the estimation department where our production accountant did the necessary coding for reimbursement, and then took any paperwork over across the lot to the department that issued the reimbursement checks. Throughout the day, I would get messages from the production office about what paperwork was where, so I could shuttle it to the next stop and or collect the checks eventually issued. Halfway through each day, another office assistant would meet me on the lot, we would exchange paperwork, and I kept at my on-lot cycling-around day. On rare downtime, and when our production was filming on the lot I would hang out on the set until called about my next pickup and drop off.

The kid in me delighted being in the studio, because I might be exchanging a passing by "hello" with Kevin Costner, Chevy Chase, or Clint Eastwood, all of whom had production offices on the lot. The second *Batman* film with Michael Keaton was under production at the time, and biking around I might see the Batmobile or one of the sets on an open soundstage. One time I came across a "stunt Batman" working on a fight sequence with another performer, and I got a front row seat.

The most magical moment for me happened one afternoon as I bicycled up from the southernmost part of the Warner Bros. lot, heading north. A soundstage's huge doors came open, and it was like television heaven had been released on earth. I saw before me in western dress a huge group of Classic Television western actors come out. Some of whom I recognized like Dubb Taylor and Robert Forster and others whom I knew by visage only. I soon found out that it was the set for the *Maverick* movie, which used a lot of those actors in that movie starring James Garner and Mel Gibson. What a kick that was. Only in Hollywood!

My only disappointment while working on Sinatra, was not getting to meet the man himself. Of the two opportunities, the first came when word came out that "Frank will be here tomorrow." Instead of my usual t-shirt, I donned a collared shirt and a tie for the occasion. Alas, a last-minute decision from Frank, who was enjoying his California sunshine in faraway Palm Springs, decided not to make the trek. There was still hope, though, as it was definite that he was going to attend the party following the end of filming the production to be held at a restaurant in downtown Los Angeles. Alas, a few days before the date, the Los Angeles riots broke out, and the event was cancelled.

As a bonus, though, Tina was ever generous when it came to obtaining tickets for her friends who wanted to see her dad live. Both at the Greek Theatre right after I worked on the show, and later at the Long Beach Arena, I got great tickets to see Frank Sinatra in concert. He was older at the time, and word was some concerts were better than others. He was a little off at the latter show, and I wonder to this day if his seeming not to recognize his opening act, Don Rickles, when the comedian came on the stage in the middle of Frank's set for a scripted part of the show, was part of the act, or a sign of Frank's age.

Oh, but at the Greek, he was on. Every note was golden, and when the singer walked from the back of the orchestra seating to the stage, it was like he was the only person in the room. Such charisma and energy. Seeing Frank Sinatra exhibit the height of his talent, from great seats in the audience is something I will never forget.

Warner Bros. My Final Home in Show Biz

In a happy turn of event Warner Bros. became my home for a while after a short hiatus to the MGM lot. As the *Sinatra* production began winding down, I began to hunt for the next gig. One connection came when I learned that Bob Rosenbaum was a Vice President for Lorimar Television on the Warner Bros. lot. Earlier in his career, he worked on *Bewitched,* and that helped to get me an interview. The Vice President on their Lorimar Culver City location, Patrick Newcomb was looking for an office assistant and one thing led to another, and I was working for the person who oversaw shows such as *Getting By*, *Step by Step*, *Perfect Strangers*, *Family Matters,* and more. I was not there a year, when Lorimar and Warner Bos. Television merged into one as the latter company, and all of the shows and offices were moved together onto the familiar-to-me Warner Bros. lot in Burbank. This studio, my favorite, became my last vocational home in my brief show business career.

Warner Bros. Television was busy, producing many projects, and that kept me engaged. Sometimes I was farmed out to other productions for one reason or another. Pilot season is a time in the winter where many potential shows were put into production by filming one episode. During pilot season I got to sometimes work as a Production Coordinator (or assistant to), which was a role that served as a conduit between the studio, production office, and the stage. I had a lot of fun and worked on pilot episodes for shows, some of which I was surprised did not get picked up.

One starred actress Teri Garr in a sitcom that took place in a tax office. Not only was she a great comedian, but the supporting cast was wonderful. These included Wallace Shawn, who people know from *The Princess Bride* movie. Watching him work was fascinating. He could take any line of dialogue and make it funny. There, I observed another actor whose style taught me something about live audience performing that no class ever offered.

The actor, Patrick Warburton, is remembered by many from his later work on *Seinfeld* as David Puddy the sometimes boyfriend of Julia Louis-Drefus' character, Elaine. On the pilot of the Terri Garr sitcom, Patrick played a security guard in the internal revenue office. One day I watched a run through and mistakenly thought this guy was awful. I watched him, and he stood in the scene like a stiff personality-less mannequin. Yet, when his line came his character came through. Later, I watched the run through, through the video monitor and recognized what he was doing. When the actor was not on camera, he simply "powered down," but before the cameras came his way, he was fully animated and in character. He exhibited a marvelous talent of being able to put his energy into reserve and bring it out fully just before it was needed I do not know if he continued to work that way, but he was also marvelous on the pilot, and I am glad I got to see how he worked at his craft.

Liking the Production Coordinator gig, I wanted to move in that direction, but none of my pilots were picked up to be made into a series, so it was back to the main television production office. I had the honor of working on *Full House* for a bit in their last season as a writer's assistant. To sit in an actual writer's room of a comedy and watch so many talented writers brainstorm over episodes was a treat. Unfortunately, they needed a seasoned third Writer's Assistant, and deserved someone of that caliber with experience. That, and the fact that the VP I had worked for, Patrick Newcomb, made them hire me did not help.

Also, while I was at Warner Bros., it only took a couple of seasons to realize that every year, *Full House* fired somebody! I began to see the writing on the wall and could tell it was either going to be me or a show production assistant named Rob. So, one day Rob and I made a deal. "If they talk about getting rid of you, the producers are going to talk about it on the writer's side of the office. If it's me, they will head over next door to your production side." We agreed to alert the other when one of us heard about the decision about who was leaving.

Rob did another really smart thing. He was great at baseball, and joined the show's softball team, which competed against other shows' teams. He was a good hitter and field player so that alone may have helped the ultimate direction. I was not surprised when he came to me one morning after I was released and gave me the bad news. As predicted, when I was not around the producers spoke openly about my not being a good fit, and they would soon tell me that I was no longer required. For reasons already shared, I cannot say that I disagreed with them. I was not up to par with what a show like theirs deserved in their eighth season. And so, I went hunting for the next! As a parting gift, Rob privately gave me a special cigar he was saving for when he sold his first script. Rob, wherever you are, let's sit down and enjoy one together some day. Your kindness, like that offered by my parents, is why I will never forget you, and the fact that I owe you a stick! Little did I know at the time that I was three seasons, and two shows away from leaving the industry.

Start at the Bottom

The Wayans Bros. was a new program starring two brothers, Marlon and Sean Wayans. The first season was gearing up, so by the time I was told that I was going to be soon let go from *Full House*, I had already lined up my next production job, and in fact ended up giving notice to *Full House*, leaving them earlier than they anticipated to begin my new position.

The Wayans Bros. was a hoot, and our offices were on the Warner Bros. Ranch, a studio up the street from the main one, which housed all of the facades for famous houses from my mother's *Father Knows Best*, to my dad's *Bewitched*. I had hope for the show's writing because the lead team of producer writers in that first season were Billy Van Zandt and Jane Milmore. I liked Billy right away. As we walked across the lot, a casual conversation led to who my father was, and he knew of my dad's contributions to his favorite show, *I Love Lucy*.

The show and the party on the lot after the show was truly something, but the ratings for it were horrible. Every week I looked, and no matter how many episodes were shown in different time slots, they always came in last place. And then fate interceded. Todd Stevens was a line producer on one of the two pilots he worked on earlier in the season. The one I worked on with him did not get picked up. My friend from the lot, Mary McLaughlin, was the production coordinator on the other one. Hers did, and so while I went briefly to *Full House*, and later to *The Wayans Brothers*, she remained working on the show about six pals who hung out together in New York. While *The Wayans Bros.* in their first season was last place in the ratings, the show she worked on, *Friends*, worked its way up to first in its initial season.

Todd phoned me one day. "Petie, my office assistant is leaving to go be a writer, and I need someone for season two, would you like to take the job?" From last to first, and it came right away with a crew jacket that gave me some local show biz street cred? Absolutely! I finished my current season and gave notice and soon began the show on which my mother had appeared a few months before!

During the first season of *Friends*, on the main Warner Bros. Studios lot, I was working up the street on *The Wayans Bros.* When my mom was cast in an episode on *Friends'* first season, I took the opportunity to drive over to visit her at work. That week my mother was playing the part of Aunt Lillian on an episode in the first season of *Friends* (1994-2004), titled "The One Where Nana Dies Twice." During rehearsals for the show, I entered onto the stage, not knowing that one year later I would be working as the assistant to the line producer, Todd Stevens, and do so for two seasons. At that point, having never seen an episode of *Friends*, I was merely entering the stage of just another show.

My timing was good as the cast had just finished a table reading of the updated script and were headed to their various dressing rooms, except for my mother and two others whom I instantly recognized. My heart leaped when I saw them. While it's rare, I can be starstruck. "Oh hi, Honey!" my mother greeted, and then she turned to the two and said, "Elliott, I'd like you to meet my son, Peter." Elliott Gould is one of my favorite actors. I am a fan of the Raymond Chandler/Philp Marlowe novels, and the films made from them. Mr. Gould gave one of my favorite portrayals as the character in director Robert Altman's *The Long Goodbye* (1973). I merely stammered a "hello" as I shook his hand. Two years later, when I was working on the show, I took the opportunity to awkwardly stammer to him that he was one of my favorite Marlowes. He sort of grunted a reply and walked away. (I was also able to tell Robert Mitchum the same thing, through a note delivered to him by his wife, whom my mother knew well. Mr. Mitchum gave me a tangible reply in the form of an autographed photo on which he wrote, "Peter, I commend your choice of mothers!") Needless to say, I preferred the latter response.

As I was leaving, my mother asked if I was going to see the show that week when it was filmed before a live audience. I told her I wasn't able to, much to her relief. Yet, my schedule opened up and I was able to sit in. "Sit me somewhere up and away, I just want to observe from afar," I informed my friend Kevin Larkin who was the Audience Coordinator for the show. Either Kevin forgot my odd request or thought he was doing me a favor, but my seat ended up being in the front row, right across from the set where my mother's scenes were filmed. Have you ever tried to will yourself invisible? I did. It did not work.

Perhaps it was the bond that she and I share in our love of music, dance, and theater. Or our years together where I helped her prepare her lines. But somehow, she sensed my presence, and perhaps it was meant to be. On this particular night, I became an ally for her. The writers and producers were frantically rewriting parts of the scene on the spot; something that happened all of the time when she co-starred on *The Odd Couple*, but this time it resulted in her lines, as written, not receiving the laugh the writers hoped for.

My mother was on stage, with me watching from the front row, as the writers and producers conferenced and came up with replacement dialogue for the cast that became increasingly unfunny. Add to that an audience that was getting tired and the laughs were not coming. At one point, she came over to me, and hovering nearby I noticed a rather pretty woman, who was drifting closer and closer to where we stood. My mother said to me, "I just don't know what to do, Peter, I am not getting any laughs," I pontificated, "Mom, it's not your fault, the line by itself is not funny, and no one can do anything with that." I noticed the woman then retreat rather quickly, and it turned out that she was one of the Executive Producers of the show. Oops. Years before, my mother would always caution me, "Be careful who you are talking to on a set, you never know who they are." Did that woman hear what I said? Most likely, but I'll never know. It just proves that first of all, mothers always know best. Secondly, there are moments where being hyperaware on film sets doesn't always lead to good things. Though my mom and I never acted together, we have the connection that between the two of us, we worked on the first three seasons of *Friends*, and what a wonderful two season adventure that show was for me.

New Pals via Friends

Getting hired on *Friends* to be the Line Producer's Assistant meant I got to work with my friend Todd Stevens. Todd was great, a workaholic, but with a joyful personality bigger than any room accompanied by an infectious laugh that often helped to lift show stresses to moments of hilarity. Another plus was the location of my workstation outside of his office, next to my friend, Mary's, so I was finally in a good place.

One thing I always have to qualify about working on *Friends* is I had mostly zero interaction with the cast, spending 90% of my week on the phone outside of Todd's office. If any cast member saw me today, they would have no idea I was one of them!

As an example, we once had rock star Chrissie Hynde from the rock band *Pretenders* on the show. As the special guest that she was, Todd and I worked carefully with her assistant in preparation for her coming onto the set. Todd wanted to offer this special guest the upmost courtesy and so he asked me to make a rare appearance on the *Friends* soundstage the morning of her and her assistant's arrival to be sure that everything in the dressing room was working and to their liking. As a fan of the band whom I had seen in concert, I was thrilled to meet Chrissie and she graciously signed a compact disc I brought as well as a program from a show I attended the year before. Chrissie was going to be in a scene with *Friends* cast member Lisa Kudrow who came up into the dressing room to meet Christie as well. Chrissie's assistant made the introduction, and turning to Lisa and pointing to me, said, "of course you two know each other." With no malice, but with her characteristic slight sneer, she looked at me, a guy she never met, and said "No, who are you?" She was the first cast member I got to introduce myself to on the set!

The first person who I met was in the production office. Mathew Perry dropped in before the second season began to say hello to producers, and he was at the time just as charming and funny as the character he played on the show. I have to say that the cast member whom I admired the most, though, was Matt LeBlanc who played Joey. Why? On show nights, after we were done filming in front of the audience, he would hang out with the crew as they broke down the sets. A small gesture like that helped all of us, who were a part of the production feel a part of the team.

And yet, despite all of the joy associated with being on a hit show and all of the perks (I could phone our Nike shoes rep and ask for a pair of sneakers and the next morning they and some t-shirts would appear on my desk), I was not happy with my vocation. I loved my family, Marie and our children, and I also loved the Episcopal parish where I worshipped, so my faith life was strong, but I soon realized that I had followed into the family business but felt unfulfilled there. I was convinced that there was something else that I was supposed to do, but I had no idea what it was. I felt that I had a good chance to remain on *Friends* for as long as the show was in production but knew I would never find my life purpose remaining on the show.

So, I made the difficult decision, when an offer came my way to work a regularly 9-5, Monday through Friday job in a commercial real estate office (in the same building outside of the Warner Bros. lot) that housed the *Friends* production offices, that I would take that simpler job as a first step in discerning what career was out there for which I had a deep passion. Thus, I gave notice at the end of our third season that I was not coming back to the show. It was the right one, I know now, but it really took a leap of faith.

Still, though, I fondly cherish my time on *Friends*. It was so much fun, and I absolutely love the people with whom I worked in the production office. The many production assistants and interns who worked with us then were lovely people. Many of them have continued on in the industry, and while some have not, we remain in touch through social media. Occasionally, I get to see some of them. Sometimes, we attend a party given by someone who worked on the show. One of my favorite gatherings was when some of us were reunited at the final cast and crew shindig which celebrated the end of the production of *Friends*.

It is a testament to the Executive Producers who made the effort to include people like me who only worked two of the many seasons of the show in the celebration. Held in a downtown Los Angeles party rental space, which used to be a hotel, it was an event like no other. Along with the other guests Marie and I had to check our cell phones in at the door. Walking in, we were greeted by the producers of the show and the head of Warner Bros Television. Near the entrance was a bar, unlike any other. The whole bar was sculpted out of ice, so you know the beverages were cold! Further back there was an outside staging area with a regular bar inside, which was outside the kitchen. In a couple of ways, I saw how those in charge of the party had, even beyond the ice bar, pulled out all the stops.

While we made our way through the gathered, making conversation with old friends, Marie and I noticed a catering employee come out of the kitchen with a tray of hors-d'oeuvres, from which we each took one of the proffered delights. Though I do not consider myself snooty, my parents raised me better than that, perhaps being one of the select few at this exclusive gathering brought it out in me. I looked at the treat on the cocktail napkin in my hand and recognizing it, I remarked, "really, little miniature Wolfgang Puck pizzas at an event like this?" I briefly assumed that in the nearby kitchen there were a bunch of store-bought frozen boxed treats being heated in the ovens. That assumption did not remain long, however, as no sooner had I made the comment, when who walked out of the kitchen wearing chef whites, but celebrity chef Wolfgang Puck himself! Marie delightedly responded, "yes, Wolfgang Puck mini pizzas made *by* Wolfgang Puck!"

Soon after Marie excused herself for a moment and I headed to the bar and grabbed another beverage, saying a brief hello to the lady sitting there. I meandered in the area, awaiting my wife's return and exchanged a glace with the woman who had turned to face me. She took a swig of her beer from the bottle and smiled at me. Though she was very attractive, I had no idea who she was. Today, my ego wants to insist that she saw something in me that she liked, but my honest self admits that she probably merely was acknowledging me. Marie returned, and we continued our mingling elsewhere. Not long after, everyone at the event went outside, where on the stage the cast and producers made a few remarks. Then, they introduced a special surprise--a rock band to entertain us. Leading it was the woman I saw at the bar, Sheryl Crow, who put on a fabulous performance!

This was another nice chance to be in touch with the show business crowd I grew up with, but by this point, I was already finding my intended vocational path. Meanwhile, my mom was finding hers, professionally and personally in these years following my dad's death and her marriage to Lou.

Mom's Semi-Retirement

Not only did I notice how the business had changed through the years from when I was on sets observing my dad and mom at work, but my own foray into the industry also confirmed the changes. With rare exceptions, the family feeling of a set was often lost. Plus, time is not kind to industry types, not only as I saw from my dad, but also how younger people becoming involved adversely affected my mom's ability to get work. Casting directors, and sometimes producers would audition her for a job, look at her resume and have no clue about what, for instance, *Father Knows Best* was!

Rather than put up with the unintended slights, my mother, due to the wealth of her work and the fact that there were people who still wanted Elinor Donahue for a role, adapted. She told her agent that she would no longer audition for anything. If the producers, however, specifically wanted her, she would come in and read. Otherwise, she declared that she was semi-retired.

Even when they wanted her, she sometimes turned down work. She did this once and understandably for Garry Marshall, with whom she worked on her *Happy Days* appearance and co-starring on *The Odd Couple*. Garry also cast her in *Pretty Woman*, introducing her to a new generation as Bridget, the "nice" saleslady who helps Julia Roberts and responds to the star's line about "he's really not my uncle," with "they never are, dear!" This one time, though, the role Garry offered was not a good fit. In his defense, he knew funny, but it was asking a lot for my mother to take the particular small part in the movie he was working on at the time. It ended up being an unsuccessful project, and the part he wanted my mother to play was a lady who sold sex toys in a shop. The joke beyond the script was seeing a nice lady talking casually about "French ticklers" and the like. This scene was not something she was comfortable with. Her deep connection to the Roman Catholic Church, which she converted to when she married Lou, weighed heavily in that decision; she couldn't perform a role like that where those in the church and friends of hers would see. So, with apologies, she turned Garry down.

After that, when new Garry Marshall projects went into production, she never got a phone call. Through a mutual friend, she reached out to Garry. Wanting to understand and rebuild a very much desired friendship again, they spoke, being honest and putting the past behind them. Luckily, it worked. She was cast in his next film, *The Princess Diaries 2: Royal Engagement* (2004), this time as a countess married to actor Tom Poston. She had nice appearances and plenty of lines strewn throughout the film, and most importantly, she had so much fun filming it. But in the end, during the final trimming of the work, all of her lines were cut. The good news is that no matter what shows up on the screen or is left on the cutting room floor, the talent's contract remains firm. This is the one movie I have watched her in where she does not say a thing. Perhaps Garry had the last laugh on that one. Just kidding. Maybe.

As mentioned, if producers wanted "Elinor Donahue," she was open to discussion, but wasn't going out there fighting for roles. This has brought a sense of serenity to her life. She will always love television and always love her career. A few years ago, she had the chance to play the role of Judge Anderson (yes, the grown-up Betty Anderson) on the Daytime Soap, *The Young and the Restless* (1973 -). It was fun. It was charming. It made her smile.

As I wrote earlier, the '90s brought many autograph show appearances, which I pushed my mother into doing in the first place. There are so many fans of Classic TV, who have dreamed of seeing her, meeting her and holding onto those memories forever, that I wanted her to be a part of it. It did take time for her to really enjoy those moments, though. While it made for nice income, it just wasn't her favorite. She's never cared for the commercial aspect of the shows, even though I remained alongside as an effervescent buffer.

I tried to convince her to accept this commercial enterprise as finally being paid back for all the times she mailed photos and supplied postage and materials at no cost to anyone else. Today, she no longer accepts requests by mail, but will very occasionally do an autograph show. Sometime in the 2010s, she was invited by Creation Entertainment to serve as one of the VIP celebrities at their event at the Rio Hotel in Las Vegas. What she loved about the *Star Trek* Convention experience in Las Vegas was that she was paid by the organizers, and thus no money exchanged hands between her and the fans. She loves her fans, and relishes these in person opportunities, but feels that the money part always gets in the way. Meeting her fans was a learning opportunity for me.

She negotiated to have a family member with her, and though she did not have to rehearse any lines, she asked me. As a fan of all things *Star Trek*, I was delighted to attend with her. Off stage and between appearances on the day she was to meet with groups, take photos, sign autographs, and be interviewed on stage by Scott Manz, there was a little downtime, and that is where I came in. Knowing both my mother and show business, I was able to either gear her up for the next segment of her celebrity day or take her mind off of it, whether we conversed about her grandchildren, memories, or sat in silence. I am glad that my show business life helps me to still be useful to hers.

I benefitted too while she was meeting with a select group of the series' fans who had paid for the privilege of intimate conversations with celebrities at the event. While my mother answered a question, I learned more about her and the characters she played. The fan asked if it was challenging for her to play a strong woman in a man's world in the *Metamorphosis* episode she did on the original series. When prompted to add my thoughts, I observed that all of my mother's characters were strong and pushed the boundaries of the time. Whether it was as Betty Anderson on *Father Knows Best* running track or competing for a class honor; or as Ellie Walker on *The Andy Griffith Show* as the first "lady pharmacist" or the first woman to run for City Council, her characters frequently pushed at the boundaries of their times.

When the *Star Trek* event concluded, I looked at her and gave her my favorite line from the original *Ocean's 11* (1960) where Peter Lawford, after hanging up from a phone call where he just asked his wealthy mother for more money, says to Frank Sinatra, "What a way to make a living!"

Will Elinor do more? Time will tell. As of the writing of this book, my mother is in her mid 80's and continues to look back fondly on her career. Though she is still delighted when opportunities come up where she and/or my dad are given recognition for their work in Classic Television, she is just as happy being retired. During the run of a play she did in 2015, she announced in every interview that this was her last performance. If true, then those of you out there who saw her as Mrs. Chumley in *Harvey* at a theater in North Carolina are, at least at this point, the last audience for whom she performed. Regardless of work, she continues in her greatest role as "mom." Even when I was well into my adulthood, she supported me, particularly when I realized my biggest personal challenge, alcohol.

A Common Enemy with my Father

There was another presence that I grew up alongside, and later lived with on my own for too long. Alcohol. I remember watching it freely enjoyed by adult imbibers, including my parents. My mother might have a vodka tonic or a glass of wine, but my dad, as I later did, drank every night. To my knowledge, he never admitted to a problem or struggle around the substance, but his history affected me. Discovering that I had a problem that needed attention convinces me that he shared the same addiction.

My first memory around alcohol was actually a pleasant one. In fact, it positively colored the imbibing of cocktails as a healthy experience. It took place in our TV room, which we referred to as, "the Den." Within this big comfortable space, with many couches and large chairs, and a warming fireplace, was a full-sized, well stocked bar in the corner. Though I can't recall if it was regular practice, I vividly remember one particular Friday evening when my parents, brothers, and I enjoyed an early evening cocktail hour. My brothers and I had all bathed and were comfy in our pajamas, slippers, and bathrobes. Dad mixed for each of us a non-alcoholic "Shirley Temple," as the sweet concoctions were called. He handed us each one in short heavy glasses, which included ice and short straws. He made a vodka tonic for Mom and concluded his evening mixologist role with a gin and tonic for himself. I downed my beverage rather quickly, and Dad acquiesced to make me another; a sign of things to come. The memory of that gathering was stamped in my mind as permeated elegance. I felt refined, comfortable, and on top of the world. It was an image that stayed with me for a long time.

Alcohol in the 1960s and 1970s was accepted at all gatherings and meals. At that time of his life, my dad drank hard liquor; gin being his choice. At some point, after we moved to the Lemp Avenue home, he swayed towards beer and wine. However, from my own experience later in life, he over-consumed those "tamer beverages." But at the time in Sherman Oaks, the "tinkling" sound of ice in his glass and the fizz of the tonic bottle when opened, like those later "glug" ones from wine poured from the large jug bottles, became part of the soundtrack in our evening home.

The first time I witnessed the adverse effects of alcohol was through my dad in that very den. It was on another evening when he allowed me to stay up much later with him as we watched a movie together. Midway through the film, I noticed as my dad slightly squirmed and groaned. I looked over at him and saw that one of his eyelids was closed while the other remained half open. Curious, I walked over to him and attempted to wake him up. "Dad?" I asked as I touched him. Like a turtle coming out of his shell, he seemed to awaken for a moment, both eyes looking almost through me, before he drifted back off. As nights like that became more frequent, I would leave and head to my own bedroom. I was always surprised to see my dad, as the man whom I knew and loved as intelligent, affable, and approachable, in that state. Then, in the morning, it was like it never happened.

Over time, I noticed that his demeanor significantly changed after he drank. If he didn't drift off, he might at best become a tad grumpy, or at the worst argumentative and bitter. With the innocence of the young, and as my daughter Amy later tried with me, I tried once to reason with him. "Dad, I don't like it when you drink. You change." Just as Amy's plea to this alcoholic was ignored, my words as a child to his father wouldn't resonate either.

It was in high school that I became convinced that he was a classic alcoholic. My health teacher passed around a brief survey for us to fill out in class. It listed ten questions, and he prompted us to answer each of them for either ourselves or someone we thought of. The topic was consumption of alcohol, and I thought immediately of my dad as I filled out the answers as if he was doing the assessment.

I answered "yes" on most of the questions: "Do you drink every night?" "Do you drink alone?" "Does your personality change when you drink?" We didn't have to hand these back, but our teacher prompted, "If you answered six out of ten of these questions with a 'yes,' you might have a problem with alcohol." The questionnaire before me on my desk had eight affirmative answers. It was then that I made a sudden, quiet proclamation, "Maybe him, but never me." That "never me," when I was in my early twenties turned into a, "I will show him how to drink like a normal person."

My one tentative attempt to bring my findings to a family member was dismissed and so I did nothing more with my knowledge that my father had a problem with alcohol, and I joined in with those around him who seemed to pretend that he did not.

My drinking began when my dad allowed me to have beer at home when I was 18. But it was when I moved into my own apartment at age 23 that my drinking started to become constant. In fact, on my first visit to the grocery store, I came home with pasta, canned sauce, bread, peanut butter, a six pack of beer, and a jumbo jug of the same wine my dad drank at the time. The soundtrack in my apartment included the "sprits" of opening the tab on a beer can, the "pop" of the cork, and the liquid "glug" as wine was poured from the bottle to the rim of my wine glass. That first night I raised the curtain on my alcoholic life. Every night my drinking was a familiarity I depended on and yet ignored. I ignored the personality changes, which included my passing out wherever I sat after the seventh or eighth glass.

My dad's drinking did change as his life continued, but it never ended. His personality changes shifted for the better when he gave up hard liquor and drank wine. Following treatments for throat cancer, he switched for a while to dark, stout beer, which he told me went down easier. The only time I knew him to go without any alcoholic beverages for an extended period of time was when he was hospitalized with pneumonia, to which he eventually succumbed, for the last thirty days of his life. It took me years to realize that others, outside of the family, also noticed this.

I realized this some years after his death in 1991, when a friend of mine at dinner overheard my dad's one-time partner, and always friend, Bill Asher, saying, "Boy, Harry really drank a lot, and he could not hold his liquor." I now wonder, as one whose alcohol consumption was quietly noticed by others; if Bill's professional separation from my dad was a result of his observations over my dad's drinking. And even though my dad had a hard enough time finding work because television moved away from the shows he produced and studios were bringing in a new generation, I believe that rumors involving his drinking may have contributed to his lack of work.

Thankfully, in the last years of his life, his tapering off allowed him to be fully present as the good-natured man I knew. Similar to him, I had a long relationship with drinking. What became abusively heavy imbibing in my twenties continued through college, into graduate school, and followed me from jobs in the television industry to ordained ministry. I drank. I drank like my dad. I drank in the evenings. My personality changed. I often passed out. Through my own battle with cancer, following surgery, and through treatment, I drank. But one day, thankfully, the opportunity for a sober life came to me.

Sobriety was offered like a life preserver. It happened in only what I can describe as a spiritual moment and didn't involve the drama one would expect around such a decision. There were no police involved, no injuries, no accidents, no courts ordering me to do something. Instead, it was a typical night where my drinking began at a local seminary's pub and concluded with me polishing off a bottle at home. I made it into bed and woke up at 3:00 a.m. My wife, Marie, was sleeping peacefully next to me, and I suddenly experienced a sensation I had not felt in a while. I was stone cold clearheaded. No fogged brain or drowsiness. I was fully awake and aware like never before. A conversation began in my head:

"I'm an alcoholic." I admitted.

"So, what does that mean?" my voice challenged back.

"It means that I am not going to drink anymore."

"How are you doing to do that?"

"I guess I'm going to go to one of those meetings."

There was no dismissing the moment. I tried to go back to sleep but this spirit within me would not let me let this moment pass. I got out of bed and went downstairs to our home office. On the computer I found the next day's meetings for a 12-Step Program. After writing down the information, I returned to bed and began rethinking my plan to attend. I tried to talk myself out of it, but I couldn't let it go. It was an early morning when I was living a life of clear honesty. I admitted to myself that if I didn't go to the 7:00 a.m. meeting, I would lose my realization. I would drink again. The lifeline was there, that morning, and I was given the option to take it or leave it. To this day, I have not regretted my decision.

I woke Marie early and shared my epiphany. With her support that morning, I left our home, drove to a local church, and walked cautiously and nervously down the steps into the brightly lit room of a church basement. There I found it full of, as I quickly discovered, people like me who craved a new life.

The hubris I once had, that I was going to show my father how to have a healthy relationship with alcohol, finally ended. I couldn't do it alone. I needed a program, and the people who were a part of it. Somehow, I was graced with the opportunity to break a cycle that had been a part of at least two generations of my family. The curtain came down on an unhealthy lifestyle that I could not deal with by myself, and a new, miraculous way of living was given to me.

Chapter 9

That's a Wrap!

What is it like being the son of a beloved actress? An example--I was going through physical therapy, and my therapist loved *Pretty Woman* and my mother's part in the film. During a session, she regaled me with the full dialogue of the scene, in-character voice. I have experienced some bizarre interactions related to my parents, but having someone imitate my mother while working on my leg muscles was just simply strange. Still, the strange is worth the satisfaction that in the industry that is often unforgiving, my parents are remembered, and shows on which they worked, or in my dad's case, helped to create, are still garnering fans today.

And what about me? Well, after *Friends*, I wrapped up my show business career. I knew from the depths within me that I was supposed to do something else. To find that something I took a job in another field. During the few years I worked in Property Management, the church I was attending was looking for someone to come on staff as a part time youth leader. I was approached for and accepted the position. I had a knack for it, and a passion for ministry began. When a full-time job opened up at that church, St. Michael & All Angels Episcopal Church in Studio City, California, I took my administrative skills and became their parish administrator as well as youth leader. And as my passion for church work continued, I wondered if I was being called to something more.

It did not take long for clergy and parishioners at the parish to ask, "have you ever thought about the priesthood?" While working these jobs, I finished my undergraduate work at California State University, Northridge, where I received my degree in Communication Studies. Simultaneously, I entered into the two-year discernment process in the Episcopal Diocese of Los Angeles and was made a postulant. For seminary, Marie and I, along with our young children, moved to Alexandria, Virginia where I attended The Virginia Theological Seminary, from where I graduated in 2007, the year I was ordained.

We settled into what I believe will be my final job in full time ministry. I serve as rector of the historic parish, Christ Episcopal Church in Chaptico, Maryland, nestled in beautiful St. Mary's County, also known by some as "God's country." When not at church, you might find me working remotely at Leonardtown Cigars, or The Toasted Foot cigar lounge, each of which adds to the small town feeling that I love so much. Our son Harry, now an adult, lives with us, and our daughter Amy works in the political world of DC, often remotely via her home in Chicago, where she will soon marry Jordan. When I travel, it is often to California, which remains a nice place to visit. And for the record, my mother and I continue the tradition which began when I first moved East. We talk on the phone every Sunday!

After a brief foray to Lodi California, where I served as rector at The Episcopal Church of St John the Baptist, Marie and I realized that we left our hearts on the East Coast, where we raised our family. Marie is a licensed sommelier (wine and spirits expert) and restaurant manager, and when her previous job invited her back, I looked for and found one nearby. We priests get to find our own jobs, apply, and interview. So, I left beautiful Lodi, in the San Joaquin Valley of California, and the good friends I made at the local cigar lounge, Stogies, and after only three years, moved back across the country.

We ended up liking Northern Virginia and the East Coast from where my dad came, and so, when I was offered a position in Virginia, I remained for a long while. First, as an associate rector at Immanuel Church on the Hill, and later a rector (head priest) in nearby Springfield Virginia at St. Christopher's. It was at these first two jobs after ordination that my show business life offered value and laughs.

One might think that my former career was wasted, but I discovered the abilities to get up in front of people and use my vocal projection techniques were a plus for the job. Also, being able to adapt to situations, such as I discovered taking an improvisation course in college helped me in situations, particularly when ministering to people with dementia. And then, there were the stories. I have used many of those included in this book in some form to help draw the listener into the message that I was preaching on a particular Sunday. Often, stories with me getting into awkward situations elicited laughter from the congregants.

At one parish, my show business affiliation led to a comedy of errors. A couple at the church confronted me with what they thought was my dual life. A website that details show business personalities as well as shows and movies mistakenly listed that the producer of a television series called *The Americans*, also named Peter Ackerman, was the son of my parents. Thus, into my office came the couple with their evidence. I showed them, through my own feeble listing on that sight, that they had it wrong. The only reason I was busy was that I was actually doing the job for which I was hired! So, yes, this is my note that I never executive produced or wrote on a series. That goes to my namesake who moved from New York to Los Angeles around the time I left the business.

My job satisfaction is truly due to her. When I became an actor, she made me promise when some other vocation took my heart, I would follow that possibility. That promise led me from the adventures recounted herein to those that continue today. Dare I admit that it was mother who knew best (see what I did there)? What a fun and satisfying life I have thus far enjoyed, and really, I acknowledge both of my parents.

After all, I grew up as the son of Harry and Elinor Ackerman. I was one of four boys living in a house in Sherman Oaks and then Studio City, California. Life was good, close to ideal, but wasn't perfect. As it shouldn't be. What was important was that our parents gifted us with love. This love that extended far outside just family. Though we enjoyed privilege in childhood, we were shown through their behaviors that while our parents were on television, that didn't put us above anyone else. And I think we turned out okay. Not spoiled. Not entitled. We were able to follow our own dreams and become successful in that which gave us joy. What more can a guy ask for?

Thank you, to Harry Ackerman and Elinor Donahue, not only for your contributions to what we now know as Classic Television, but also for raising me in your most important roles, husband and wife, Dad and Mom, classically marvelous parents.

The National Academy
of
Television Arts and Sciences

Presents this Certificate to

Elinor Donahue

"Father Knows Best"

in Recognition of

Nomination

for the

Best Supporting Actress
in a Comedy Series
(Continuing Character)

For the Awards Period
January 1, 1958 to February 28, 1959

Harry S Ackerman
President

MEMO
HARRY ACKERMAN

www.ingramcontent.com/pod-product-compliance
Lightning Source LLC
Chambersburg PA
CBHW071415150726
48000CB00001B/330